Model Essays

OCR GCE Religious Studies

H573 Philosophy of Religion, Ethics & Christian Thought

Peter Baron Andrew Capone & Daniella Dunsmore

Published by Active Education,

First published in 2018

ISBN: 9781980289869

Cartoons used with permission © Becky Dyer

All images © their respective owners

Links, reviews, news and revision materials available on www.peped.org

www.peped.org website allows students and teachers to explore Philosophy of Religion and Ethics through handouts, film clips, presentations, case studies, extracts, games and academic articles.

Pitched just right, and so much more than a text book, here is a place to engage with critical reflection whatever your level. Marked student essays are also posted.

Contents

Introduction

The aim of this book is to subject essays done under timed conditions to deep marking. Deep marking means that a comment is made on every paragraph and the grade awarded is fully justified and explained. In other words - it is the kind of detailed marking that full time teachers inevitably never have the time and opportunity to do. Eleven essays are of A* level; eight more of A grade level.

Every student needs guidance in essay-writing under timed conditions, because it a skill we can learn and develop. However, as a general guidance the examiner is looking for four things: clarity, balance, coherence and a comprehensive, critical discussion of the essay title. We need to imagine taking a hammer to the title, smashing it into pieces and then re-assembling it as a conclusion.

In this process of taking a title apart we need to do a number of things:

a. Turn the title into a one-line thesis statement.

b. Justify that thesis statement with a strong analysis and evaluation of different viewpoints.

c. Correctly identify philosophers past and present to use in your points and counter-points (but not too many, or it will be a list).

d. Remember to present a line not just on the technical vocabulary, but the trigger words like 'Discuss" and "Critically Compare", and the words in between such as 'is more useful than'. Useful to whom and for what?

e. Try to say something interesting, either by using an unusual example or by presenting a philosophical idea, such as a paradox. A paradox is an apparent contradiction which you can go on to explain. "Paradoxically, Dawkins in the *God Delusion* presents a classic straw man argument. He paints a distorted picture of Christianity to knock down as a 'straw man', and does so by something (for a scientist) profoundly unscientific. He selects only the bad bits to comment on, and says nothing about the good".

Before we start you will need a copy of the specification which you can download from the OCR website. I would recommend downloading just the pages relevant to your papers (you will have three papers to do). Then you will need *two copies.*

The first copy staple together and keep to hand for reference. The second copy cut into sections, and then stick each section at the front of the relevant part of your notebook or folder of notes.

Then take a highlighter pen and highlight any words or phrases you don't understand, and any authors named you haven't studied, or you don't feel familiar with.

It's surprising how much confidence you will gain from getting organised and having a system in place that moves you closer to top grade. Then use this book as guidance on how to hit a top level mark (Level 6). Once you have the feel, then all that remains is to practise under timed conditions. You have two hours to do three questions.

How Essays are Marked and Graded

Essays are marked according to levels and then graded according to distribution of the marks of every candidate. So for example, the top 3% of candidates will get A*. It is therefore impossible to say with certainty from year to year what so-called 'raw mark', when turned into a percentage, will gain a grade A.

The Levels

There are six levels of mark, and within each level a band of marks. Here I am focusing just on the top level, which is Level 6.

The AO1 criteria at level 6 reads as follows for a mark range of 14-16:

An excellent attempt to address the question showing understanding and engagement with the material; excellent ability to select and deploy relevant information. Extensive range of scholarly views, academic approaches, and/or sources of wisdom and authority are used to demonstrate knowledge and understanding.

Notice how the word 'excellence' needs to be fully understood. This is what this book of model essays is designed to help you understand - you need to 'see' how AO1 excellence is represented in five ways.

1. Excellent ability to address the question.

2. Excellent understanding and engagement with the material.

3. Excellent selection and deployment of the material.

4. Excellent range of scholarly views and academic resources.

5.   Excellent understanding.

These five forms of excellence are testing part of what are called 'knowledge and understanding skills'. These combine with AO2 analytical skills which involve the ability to unpack ideas, clarify them, order them in a logical sequence, and fit them together in a way that is coherent - an analytical argument starts somewhere, hangs together and concludes somewhere. You know an excellent analysis because it is 'strong' or 'clear' or 'convincing'. AO1 skills are particularly concerned with selection, engagement, range and understanding. Analytical skills are listed in AO2.

The AO2 criteria at level 6 reads like this, for 21-24 marks:

An excellent demonstration of analysis and evaluation in response to the question. Confident and insightful critical analysis and detailed evaluation of the issue. Views skilfully and clearly stated, coherently developed and justified. Excellent line of reasoning, well-developed and sustained, which is coherent, relevant and logically structured.

Notice how the emphasis has shifted to evaluation with analysis. Evaluation is when an idea or an argument is weighed up and subjected to criticism. The argument may have weaknesses. The examiner is looking for a 'line of reasoning' which is 'coherent, relevant and logically structured'. Analysis and evaluation are woven into the fabric of the essay as it proceeds, building on AO1 understanding and selection.

So AO2 criteria are concerned both with evaluation and higher order analytical questions of logic and structure. There's a full table of all the levels and how to interpret them at the back of the book.

Your grade

In your exam for each paper, you have to write three essays out of a choice of four. Each essay is marked out of a maximum of 40 marks. The total for each paper is therefore 120 marks and for the whole exam, 360 marks. You have a maximum *40 minutes for each essay.*

When all the marks are in, the distribution of marks for all candidates is divided up to give the grades awarded. Usually an A* is 90% and over, an A grade 80% and over, with other grades forming bands of 10%.

But just to illustrate the point: in the first exam of the new specification, the AS level exam of 2017, A grade was awarded for 73% and over, and B grade 63% and over.

How experienced examiners mark

Experienced examiners tend to read the essay through first, trying to get a feel of whether the question is properly understood, unpacked and addressed, and then in their minds they intuitively place it in a broadly A, B etc grade boundary. They then read it through applying the AO 1 and AO2 levels. If these two parts of the process are out of line, they read through a third time and try to make sure there is a consistency between the parts of the answer and the feel of the whole essay.

We can be confident of one thing: this new specification is not designed to be harder. So any teacher reading this should make sure that the grade they are giving students is close in standard to grades given in the previous specification. If this isn't the case, it is likely we are marking too harshly - which is a common problem.

How this book works

This selection of essays aims to cover every section of the syllabus and to give clear guidance on how these different levels are applied in real examples, done under timed conditions as far as possible.

We have not just included A* answers as we are eager to show you how you can drop a grade quite easily by ignoring an aspect of the question, or perhaps by having an answer that is unbalanced. Sometimes students are simply too timid to have a strong analytical line or to impose some sense on a question. Timidity will never produce excellence.

Of course there are different ways to structure an answer and different tactics can be employed to achieve the same end. Some of these different approaches are discussed in my book, *How to Write Philosophical Essays* which goes into greater detail on points of structure, coherence and logic.

Finally, we use examples here from Ethics, Philosophy of Religion and Christian Thought. Other paper options are not addressed here.

Philosophy of Religion H573/1

An A* candidate in Philosophy of Religion will understand, analyse and evaluate how the metaphysical idea of God is justified and experienced historically, and in contemporary culture, and how the 'ghosts' (as secularism writer Charles Taylor calls them) of Christianity still echo through the writings and ideas of people today. So we are examined on:

1. Traditional arguments for the existence of God. These have been adapted in various ways by contemporary theologians such as Professor John Hick, Richard Swinburne, and Anthony Kenny.

2. Traditional arguments about Religious Experience and Religious Language, which overlap other parts of the syllabus as they are both targets of Enlightenment thinkers such as David Hume.

3. The philosophical roots of such questions in Plato and Aristotle. These two writers dominate our syllabus and again, there are synoptic links to be made, for example, between Plato's forms, Kant's idea of the noumenal and Hick's use of Kant's noumenal in his theory of Universal Pluralism (in the Christian Thought paper).

Notice too how the metaphors introduced by the Greeks echo through history and into our own age. Plato's charioteer with its picture of reason trying to control the twin horses of our passions and our ideals resonates with Freud's theory of human consciousness and the conscience (Ethics) or Augustine's depiction of human nature as fundamentally conflicted by sin (Christian Thought). Are human beings fundamentally good or fundamentally bad? This underlying question is everywhere in our syllabus - natural law theorists argue 'fundamentally good' (we share in synderesis, the innate desire to do good, irrespective of our commitment to God) but Augustine shares Paul's view that we are deeply corrupted by original sin.

Finally, there is a very big outstanding question we address in Philosophy of Religion. Does a belief in metaphysics actually need God at all? And if we need God to make sense of metaphysical reality (truth, beauty, love, justice) then which depiction of God do we find acceptable?

So if we keep these bigger question in our mind, such as what it means to be human, the place of metaphysics in human experience, the origin of right and wrong, and the purpose of life, I think the syllabus makes more sense and we begin to see synoptic links (that is, link between papers and across history).

And even (this is a higher order skill) we can become culture readers, able to see these ghosts rearing up in our own culture, presenting us with examples, and demanding us to answer this question: is God, as Nietszche suggests, really dead?

And if not 'dead' then perhaps in some sense 'true'?

Note: in the marked essays that follow, our comments are in this italicised font.

'Episteme comes from reason, not doxa.' Discuss (34/40 Grade A)

Plato, a Greek philosopher, believed that episteme, true knowledge, came from reason. He believed doxa came from experiencing the world, which he believed in fact gave humans the true knowledge they seek. His student, Aristotle believed doxa was the first step in gaining true knowledge as it existed in the physical world. Through Plato's theory of the FORMs, I believe episteme comes from reason, and this is how we gain true knowledge.

This is an excellent introduction showing the different points of view on the question about the origin of knowledge. The candidate identifies that Plato favoured reason while Aristotle argued from experience. The candidate has also shown what the line of reasoning will be in this essay: the Platonic thesis. The essay should therefore argue towards that rationalist perspective and conclude likewise.

Plato's main theory is that of the World of FORMs. Plato states that the World of FORMs is recognisable by humans as our souls transmigrated. Before reincarnating, our souls were able to recognise the true FORMs before we forgot them in our earthly bodies. Plato describes the World of FORMs as unchangeable. This is backed up by philosopher Parmenides who says "The world is unchangeable". Plato states we can experience the examples of the FORMs in our earthly bodies. Those who do not understand the FORMs however will say there are different types of tree. Plato condemns this type of thinking and says we in fact recognise the examples of the perfect FORM of tree-ness. In the allegory of the cave, the free prisoner symbolises the attainment of true knowledge by recognising the true FORMs when escaping the cave. The shadows watched by the other prisoners is not the true reality, however they believe this is true reality as this is what they experienced. This illustrates that Plato's ideas of attaining true knowledge through the FORMs and not by the examples we see in the temporal world. Therefore, episteme comes from reason.

The candidate has reviewed Plato's perspective by commenting upon his approach to FORMs, how we perceive FORMs in the temporal world and how it is reflected in Plato's Cave allegory. Given the time constraints of an essay, only 40 minutes, it is impossible to detail everything, so the candidate must sacrifice great depth to cover all points. Here the candidate has shown an understanding of the FORMs, the cave and influences on Plato. The candidate then links back to the question by showing that this approach shows that episteme comes from reason.

Aristotle challenges Plato's theory however by presenting the 'Third Man' theory. Because the FORM of 'man' is a man itself, surely there must be a FORM for the FORM of a man. This challenges Plato's theory, as it demonstrates infinite regression. Aristotle challenges his teacher further by stating that the World of FORMs cannot be proved as it relies on reincarnation. The World of FORMs is not in the temporal world meaning there is no empirical proof of it. Aristotle's challenges show that not only is true knowledge gained by doxa, but episteme does not come from reason.

The candidate has attempted to undermine Plato by presenting the Third Man Fallacy which has been done fairly well, though some additional explanation would be better. The challenge from the evidence for reincarnation could be better emphasised. The candidate has missed the challenge that Plato's argument implies a FORM for everything, even one-legged-pirates. This reductio ad absurdum is a good challenge to use against Plato.

However, it should be noted that Plato's theory only applies to abstract notions such as love, justice and maths are the true FORMs, not necessarily physical object. Aristotle questions if there are FORMs for everything such as a sick dog or a three-legged cat. Plato however is supported by Pythagoras. Pythagoras' theorem states abstract notions such as maths do not exist in the temporal world but in fact there is a perfect FORM of it in the world of FORMs. He also states that all things are static and unchanging, suggesting that the World of FORMs and the FORMs are perfect and eternal. Plato is also supported by Heraclitus who says that "You can never step in the same river twice" and the world is constantly in flux. This signifies that humans cannot experience the world the same way twice, indicating that true knowledge is eternal e.g. maths cannot come from experience. From the support of philosophers and examples, episteme comes from reason.

The candidate managed to refer back to the reductio ad absurdum challenge in the response to Aristotle's challenge. This is a very good response identifying that Plato's theory only works with abstraction notions rather than everyday things.

Aristotle's approach to attaining knowledge by experience challenges Plato, however. Aristotle emphasised the value of studying the physical world and this approach is empirical. His theory of the four causes also question Plato's theory. Aristotle believed that everything is related to having four causes. This included matter, form, their efficient cause and their final cause; telos. An example of this is a wax stamp the matter if the wax stamp is the stamp itself while the form is what it is made of. The actuality of the wax stamp is what actually, physically it is, and the potentiality is what it could become, in this case a seal for a letter. This reason illustrates that all things have a purpose and the potentiality of it is effect. Aristotle's four causes perhaps shows that experiencing the world and observing it with and empirical approach will improve it. Therefore, episteme does in fact come from experience.

The candidate has overviewed Aristotle's theory of causes, and given particular attention to matter and form. The wax stamp is an excellent example to use. It is always a good idea to use the scholars' own examples. Another would be the bronze statue showing bronze matter, in the statue form, created by the sculptor with the purpose of honouring the gods. The link back to the question might have been better emphasised: that we know the world through this empirical approach rather than from the armchair.

In response to this, Aristotle's mistakes questions if his observations are true. *A better way of stating this would be 'Aristotle's errors in observation bring into question the reliability of empiricism as a source of knowledge.'* He stated that women are deformed and have fewer teeth than men and in this time, society as patriarchal. Aristotle also states that people who aren't smart were born to be slaves. He believed that they are unable to control themselves and should be enslaved which we would not accept as truthful.

This should be rounded up and a mid-conclusion should be drawn, then linked back to the question as the next part of the paragraph is on a different aspect of the response to Aristotle.

Democritus, a Greek philosopher believed that if a rock was continuously cut into to, a piece would be so tiny that it could no longer be divided. He called this a-toms and believed they were eternal. A-toms in atoms however was a failure as atoms can be divided into protons, neutrons and electrons. This shows that experience just gives changing opinion and episteme comes from reason, further supported by the change in physics from Newtonian mechanics to Quantum physics.

This is an excellent challenge against Aristotle as it shows that reason established what empiricism never managed to achieve, an understanding of the theory of non-divisibles. This conclusive point should be made clear and linked back to the question.

Plato's theory of the FORMs shows that the attainment of true knowledge does in fact comes from episteme as experiencing and observing the world can result to changing opinion. The World of FORMs illustrates that everything we experience now is primarily not the true reality and only our souls can experience the World of FORMs. Aristotle's statement of observing the world to gain knowledge is questionable as we can "never step in the same river twice" meaning the word cannot be experienced the same way, therefore people's knowledge may be different, therefore episteme comes from reason.

Overall: 34/40 Grade A

The candidate has shown how the reasoning and responses to the challenges of the essay have come to the point where Plato's perspective is the more believable. The use of supporting scholars throughout have helped to draw that conclusion so it is unsurprising, though validly done, that this conclusion is drawn.

AO1 13/16

The candidate has shown a very good breadth and some good depth of knowledge. The use of additional scholars is an excellent way of showing a wider understanding of the topic and the context of the theories. Some additional depth in Plato's theory of FORMs and Aristotle's Causes might have been worth investing.

Further, the candidate showed a good nuanced selection of knowledge concerning additional scholars and Aristotle's weaknesses.

AO2 21/24

The candidate challenges Plato and then responds to the challenges very well. All challenges are resolved so that the conclusion is expected but balanced. All arguments are developed well and justified with evidence and scholarly opinion which is excellent.

The line of reasoning begins in the introduction and continues all the way through to the conclusion. This is exactly what should appear in an essay. The thesis statement in the introduction should sign-post where the essay will go and it should all come to a final conclusion validly argued and demonstrated in what has been presented.

The cosmological argument successfully demonstrates that God must exist. Grade A 32/40

The cosmological argument is arguably one of the most controversial topics debated by philosophers since Aristotle and Plato, and further by Thomas Aquinas within the Summa Theologica. During this period, the cosmological argument distanced itself from the existence of God by religious argument, and rather attempted to prove the creation of the universe through seemingly scientific reason.

An interesting way to interpret the value of the cosmological argument as a sort of scientific proof for God's existence. There should be a thesis statement here to show the reader where the essay will go and what to expect in the conclusion.

Aquinas' arguments in the Summa Theologica (sum of all theology) support the cosmological argument in his 'Five Ways'. *A moment is always worth sparing just to consider the gravity of what St Thomas Aquinas' title of his work means: the sum of all theology. This is a real milestone in human understanding of God and Aquinas draws from Greek Philosophy and Judeo-Christian theology to attempt a complete understanding of God. While we might disagree on the soundness of his conclusions, it cannot be disputed that this work is second to none in its thoroughness and even now all our discourse in theology is somehow connected to something Aquinas said.* His first way was focused on motion, and he stated that motion is observable; that everything moves from a state of potentiality to actuality, such as wood is potentially hot but actually cold, and the fire is actually hot, and since it is in a state of actuality, it can move the wood from being potentially hot, to actually hot. Aquinas uses this example to show 'God' as the first mover (adapted from Aristotle's 'prime mover'), stating that God is pure actuality. Within this way, Aquinas states that motion cannot go on infinitely. However, this was argued by Hume against the cosmological argument, stating that if infinite regression is possible in maths (i.e, pi), it is possible elsewhere, therefore inferring that there may be no 'first mover'.

This is a good explanation of motion, linked to Aristotle and justified using the example of the wood and fire. The attack on infinite regression is an important point to make. If one motion stems from another there are only two possible explanations, infinite regression or first motion.

This argument of infinite regression when discussing the existence of 'God' by the cosmological argument is also continued in Aquinas' second way from causality. Aquinas argues that every effect must have a cause; a theory which is demonstrated by scientific method (however nothing can be proven with certainty) as the effect of a child was caused by parents, as the effect of the universe was caused by God. Furthermore, this shows that nothing can come from nothing, as philosopher Leibniz said, "ex nihilo nihil fit" (from nothing, nothing comes), and since everything is around us, it must've been caused by something; the first cause, i.e, God.

This is another good paragraph, furthering Aquinas' ways with causation. It would be worth linking back to Heraclitus who argued the point that 'nothing comes from nothing.'

This is further challenged by Kant, *(further challenged? It has not been challenged yet so this cannot be further challenge but an initial challenge in this essay)* who said that cause and effect only logically occur in the spatio-temporal world, and to discuss and debate on causality outside of that would be illegitimate. Hume also debated against this with his seventh, and final criticism, *(a worthwhile observation is that when we are learning or researching challenges and theories they may well be numbered and categorised in a particular way, but in their original forms they are not categorised in this way. It would be* more advisable to identify the challenges as simply challenges, and not categorise them as contemporary scholars might) implying that we, as humans, infer a cause, such as when we hail a bus, it is not really us that stops the bus, but rather the driver themselves. As we can never experience causality, it is impossible to infer what we cannot know, which in the cosmological argument is that God is the first cause. Hume's argument was also developed from the argument created by William of Ockham, who queried whether there was a necessary link between cause and effect at all, thus, questioning if there is a link between the universe and God/'first cause' itself, especially with Leibniz's principle of sufficient reason, which theorises that every contingent fact of the world must have an explanation, such as the contingent universe.

The candidate makes some good challenges here, referring to Hume, Kant and Leibniz. The problem is that the candidate does not draw a final conclusion here, arguing that causation is misguided and unverifiable. It would be wise to link back to the thesis statement here. This is why it would be advisable to have a thesis statement, so that the paragraph can link to the candidate's thesis.

Lastly is Aquinas' third way for the argument for God's existence; necessity. Aquinas categorised everything into two; necessary, and contingent (such as a child is contingent on their parents to exist, causing the parents to become necessary), the universe is contingent on something, since without the universe, there would be nothing. Aquinas perceived this to be God, thus, making God pure necessity, since God is not contingent and in the same way a purely actual thing can move a potential substance into actuality, God made the universe contingent.

This is a good overview of the argument from contingency, however, since the candidate will later challenge it with Russell, it would have been worthwhile supporting the third way with Copleston.

Bertrand Russell argued against this in his 1948 BBC radio debate with Father Frederick Copleston. Russel, an atheist (albeit with some seemingly agnostic views),argued that simply because man has a mother, does not mean mankind has a mother, and further that the word "necessary" cannot be used in anything other than a certain analytical proposition, of which he argued the existence of something was not. Copleston challenged this, arguing that to say that something was brought into existence by another thing already in existence is an analytical proposition itself; that the world is aggregate, thus, proving us as contingent, meaning that something necessary must have created us, hence proving the existence of God.

The presentation of Russell is good, though the candidate should have presented Copleston first and presented his version of the argument, that everything needs a sufficient reason. This way Russell's challenge would have made more sense. The candidate should emphasise Russell's challenge that a sufficient reason is unnecessary in explaining why things are the way they are. The candidate might have used Russell's example of the match: that the cause of the match is the striking against the box and nothing more.

In conclusion, although the cosmological argument was, and still is highly debated upon, to say that the current cosmological argument proves the existence of God would be insufficient since we cannot infer the existence of God or the creation of the universe as we will never know. Although Aquinas' ways are well-supported arguments for the existence of God, and approach it almost scientific, as a theologian himself, his arguments are biased in the support for the cosmological argument. Alternatively, Hume's contrasting challenges are thoroughly developed with sufficient reasoning, however we cannot know what is inferenced by us as beings, thus, proving that the cosmological argument can never successfully demonstrate that God must exist, nor prove that he does not for we cannot infer what we do not know out of the spatio-temporal world.

Overall 32/40 Grade A

This is a very summative conclusion bringing together the different arguments presented, and drawing a final conclusion. The candidate has recognised the importance of Aquinas' arguments, but has been convinced by the logical responses by Kant and Hume. One way of responding to them would be to consider Aquinas' approach not so much as a logical argument for God, but rather as an observation that, as Heidegger asked "why is there something rather than nothing?" Despite Hume's and Kant's dislike for the inference of a cause for the world, the reality is that there is a world and everything in it needs accounting for,, so Aquinas argues that we account for the world by the existence of God.

AO1 13/16

The candidate has shown excellent knowledge, with development, and depth. However, the candidate might have developed the use of Copleston to support Aquinas. Additionally, the candidate might have mentioned Peter Kreeft's explanation of the argument and the example of the borrowed book.

The candidate does select excellent knowledge, especially in response to the argument from causation, especially with Hume's and Kant's challenges.

AO2 19/24

The candidate answers the question directly and accurately referring back to the question regularly, though not following it by a reference in every paragraph, which would have been better. Arguments are analysed and evaluated throughout excellently.

The conclusion is excellent. However, it would have been better if the candidate had offered a thesis statement in the introduction so that it was clear where the essay would go from the outset.

Assess the extent to which the ontological argument fails to prove that God exists analytically. (32/40 Grade A)

The ontological argument was presented by *St* Anselm, the monk and Archbishop. He wanted to find a way to prove God's existence analytically which is something that would be self-contradictory to deny. Synthetically is something that has to be explored to know. *Check how analytic and synthetic are used as terms: 'synthetic truths' are things that require evidence to demonstrate.* The ontological argument attempts to prove God's existence through definition. *Better, would be 'The ontological argument attempts to prove God's existence analytically, or a priori'.* Anselm and Descartes agree, whereas Aquinas, Gaunilo and Kant do not. *Since the candidate has already mentioned that the ontological argument is St Anselm's creation, it would make more sense in this part of the introduction to assert that Descartes agrees with Anselm.* I also disagree with this argument as I do not believe it achieves its goal.

The candidate has made clear direction that the essay will go, in opposition to St Anselm and Descartes. A reason was also given which informs us of what we are looking for in this essay.

Anselm presents his definition of God as that than which nothing greater can be conceived. So therefore God must exist, even the fool understands God's definition. The candidate should have saved this conclusion until after the painter and the next premise had been explained. They are a fool for understanding the definition then denying God's existence. Anselm uses the painter as an example. If a painter imagines a painting that has yet to be created it is not as great as a painting that has already been created. This is not quite correct, St Anselm us suggesting that the 'idea' of the painting that exists only in the painter's imagination (before it is painted) is not as great an idea as the 'idea' of the painting that exists in the painter's imagination and reality (after it has been painted). It is a comparison of ideas. It is greater to exist in reality and the mind than the mind alone. To be necessary is greater than to be contingent. To be contingent is to rely on something else to exist and to not have to exist. Whereas God doesn't rely on something else to exist and it has to exist. So therefore God must exist analytically. This is correct. The candidate should have explained St Anselm's second version of the argument as well; that being that it is greater to exist necessarily than contingently, therefore God must be necessary.

Guanilo challenged Anselm as although he was a monk, he did not believe that you can prove God's existence analytically but rather that God reveals himself to us. Good distinction between the positions of Gaunilo and St Anselm. Guanilo argued that Anselm merely assumes that we all accept his definition of God, which we do not. He uses the example of the rumour. Someone can describe a person to you in such detail that you can picture that person in your mind. That does not mean that they exist. Also he presented the perfect island example. If someone was to describe an island to you in such detail it appeared perfect and you can picture it in your mind and understand it. That does not prove that this island exists. Guanilo accuses Anselm of moving from de dicto necessity to de re necessity, which is illogical. You cannot define God into existence.

This may seem a brief paragraph but the candidate has said everything that is necessary to explain Gaunilo's position including the two examples: rumour and island. Additionally, the candidate has presented the 'de dicto'/'de re' distinction. Perhaps the candidate might have analysed this a little further or used Aristotle to support it: it is the mark of the educated mind to be able to entertain a thought without accepting it. Anselm assumes that when we understand the idea of God as that than which nothing greater can be conceived, that we automatically accept it. Ironically, Aristotle's statement suggests that if we were to automatically accept it, then and only then would we be the fool.

Aquinas also disagreed with the ontological argument. He argued that God is subjective, and there is not one agreed on definition of God. *One should always be a little careful with assertions. Clearly the candidate did not mean that 'God is subjective' but rather 'the definition of God is subjective'.* Therefore God's definition itself is contingent as it can vary from person to person. We do not know God's nature, so therefore we can only show God to exist synthetically. If we were to know God's nature or essence then we would be able to know that he is analytic and necessary. *Again, be careful with the use of the term 'analytic'. It is not that we know God is analytic but rather that we can know God analytically.* However God's nature or essence is beyond our comprehension so we will not be able to discover it. Therefore if we were to know God's nature we would discover that it is necessary and analytic, however we cannot as there is an epistemic distance between us and God, so God can only be shown to exist synthetically in the ontological argument.

Excellent use of the term 'epistemic' to emphasise the reason why we cannot know God analytically, as God is so beyond the human mind.

Descartes was a supporter of Anselm and the ontological argument. His version of the argument argues that just as a triangle has three sides, and how a mountain has to have a corresponding valley, God must exist. This is a little premature a sentence. The triangle and mountain examples should be saved until after the premises of the argument have been presented and explained. Existence is a predicate of God, so he must exist analytically. Good. This is the argument. Descartes argued that 'God is the sum of all perfection' and is the only prefect being. Therefore Gaunilo's 'perfect island' example is no longer valid, as the island is not a 'perfect' island in the same way that God is 'perfect'. Therefore God must exist analytically. The candidate should have asserted that to Descartes, God's existence does not need to be proven but discovered, in the same way that we discover that triangles have three sides; likewise, God's existence is a matter analytic logic, in the same way that the mountain necessary has a valley, God necessarily has existence.

Kant opposed the ontological argument. He argued that 'all existential propositions are synthetic' meaning that everything that is true or not must have evidence to back it up. To prove something exists you have to find examples of it and instantiate it. To discover something's predicates, you must first instantiate it. Then look for predicates, therefore existence cannot be a predicate. Russell uses the example of 'cows exist' this statement is saying that the idea of cows has been instantiated and shown to exist. Frege also uses an example, 'tame tigers exist', 'exist' is not giving us any further knowledge of tigers it is just telling us that they have been instantiated. If God is beyond out space and time, we cannot prove his existence analytically.

There is a danger that this paragraph jumps about from one scholar to another. While all three are arguing similar things and can certainly be connected together, the candidate has not spent a great deal of time detailing their points. All that the candidate asserted is correct, but not analysed very deeply. This is evidence of breadth over depth.

Anselm and Descartes both support the ontological argument through theories such as God's definition meaning he has to exist, and how existing is a predicate of God. However Aquinas, Kant and Gaunilo opposed the argument through arguments such as needing to instantiate something before discovering its predicates and how there is no one agreed on definition of God and even if there were, there would be no way of knowing if we were correct or not. In conclusion, I do not believe that the ontological argument proves God's existence analytically.

32/40 Grade A

It would have been worth the candidate finishing with a supporting reason, e.g. 'In conclusion, I do not believe that the ontological argument proves God's existence, as God cannot be instantiated and all existential propositions need instantiating.' However, this conclusion was summative and covered both sides of the argument, which was good.

AO1 12/16

The candidate has shown very good knowledge and understanding of the topic. There is some good breadth and depth, though some analysis could have been done to a greater degree. The candidate has used a good variety of arguments, though the second version of St Anselm's ontological argument should have been mentioned.

AO2 20/24

The candidate has used a good variety of scholars to challenge the position of the ontological argument, has shown good development and justified positions with examples and quotes. There is a good use of vocabulary to emphasise arguments and a good breadth of knowledge of how the argument can be challenged. Some scholars could have been given additional analysis.

To what extent can it be believed that religious experiences are no more than illusions? (39/40 Grade A*)

The veridicality of religious experiences is a contentious philosophical issue, sparking scholarly debate from William James, Sigmund Freud and the like. It is imperative first to address what constitutes a religious experience; Rudolph Otto famously proclaimed them to be an "apprehension of the wholly other." In other words, religious experience is best articulated as having experienced a spiritual presence external to oneself. Recorded in a variety of forms, whether it be visions or voices, these experiences are often asserted to be illusory - the aforementioned Freud strongly advocates this notion, claiming that the phenomena known as 'religious experience' is merely a construct of the psyche, devoid of any divine authorship whatsoever. The debate is unequivocally clear.

The introduction is written superbly with a high level of vocabulary. The candidate identifies the topic under examination and lays out the parameter to be discussed in the essay. A clear thesis statement would be better, however, this introduction suggests that the direction of the essay is to critique religious experience.

William James outlined his thesis concerning religious experience in 'The Varieties of Religious Experience: A Study in Human Nature.' It can be extrapolated from James' work that religious experiences are not illusions, despite being 'psychological phenomena'. It is vital to present the characteristics James accredited to religious experience to give further insight into his thesis. These include that religious experiences are passive and thus not willed by the individual, contrary to the assertions made by Freud; furthermore, ineffability is another notable aspect of the experience according to James, it being that the recipient cannot articulate their experience. James argued vehemently that the passivity of the experience elevates its credibility, implicating perhaps the intervention of the divine. Added to this, the noetic, revelatory nature of the experience appears to contravene the notion that religious experiences are illusions; James postulated that the 'good disposition' of the knowledge revealed points to the existence of what he called 'something larger' This concept can be corroborated with reference to Teresa of Avila, whom argued that a 'religious experience' is only 'religious' if the recipient is left feeling at peace; this is analogous to James' insistence for a 'good disposition'.

The candidate has explored the views of James and linked it to thoughts by Avila, very good knowledge, however, it is unclear to what end they are included. It is not linked back the question directly and so we are left wondering why it was included at this stage.

Subsequently, it should be reiterated that James vouched for the notion that religious experiences are 'psychological phenomena.', for it is evident that he meant this to denote how the propensity to have an experience is universally accessible, provided one tunes their mind to the divine. In fact, James references Indian Yogi as an example of how the mind can be made more receptive to religious experience. Thus, with this in mind, one can refute the often cited counter that religious experiences are illusory given the fact that not all people receive them.

It would have been wise to include this paragraph with the previous one as it shows where James' views lie and how it answers the question that religious experiences do happen and are not illusion. However, it should be noted that the inclusion of the four characteristics need to be explained as part of James' qualification for whether or not an experience is "religious", and genuine, as opposed to illusory, and then it should be stated that James recorded many examples of these experiences, adding evidence to the case in point.

Contrary to this, the psychological challenge to religious experience - Freud its chief proponent – asserts that religious experiences are no more than illusions, constructed by the psyche most fundamentally to satisfy neuroses. Freud's challenge is derived from his analysis of mentally ill patients at Saltpetre hospital, wherein ritualistic behaviour was demonstrated. It was asserted by Freud that this ritualistic behaviour was comparable to religious practices; the most notable of which he claimed were routine prayer and worship. Controversially, the culmination of Freud's deductions produced the infamous assertion that religion "is comparable to a childhood neurosis." For Freud, religious experiences are illusory, stemming from an innate desire for a father figure; interestingly, he draws the connection between this and the widely known monotheistic Christian God. Teresa of Avila's reported religious experience, of being thrust by a 'Golden spear', can arguably be explained using the apparatus inherent to Freud's psychoanalytical theories. It could be plausible to suggest in line with Freud's line of thinking that Avila's celibacy – her repressed sexual desires (as a nun) – manifested themselves into a euphemistic representation of a phallus ('Golden spear'). One must acknowledge though that the means by which these conclusions are extrapolated is completely speculative, based on nothing more than conjecture. The example of Avila must be treated with caution, since Freud himself is not the author of this particular theory.

The candidate has made a very interesting link between Freud's own views on neurosis and a way of interpreting Teresa of Avila's ecstasy. The candidate has been careful to note that this is a speculative interpretation; however, it certainly does use what is taken to be a specifically religious experience and use it to ironically undermine itself.

In spite of this however, the psychological challenge and its subsequent assertions can be refuted on the grounds that Freud's thesis is highly abstract, underpinned by what Dr Karl Popper to be a pseudo – science. *This is a good synoptic link between religious experience and religious language.* In extension of this point, Freud's psychological challenge cannot be accepted as truth, *(it would be more pertinent to say that it cannot be accepted as conclusive proof but rather speculation)* since the psyche is a phenomenon that is still not understood fully today. Irrespective of whether our anatomical understanding is sound, the evidence proposed by Timothy O' Leary implicates the difficulty one has in accepting the veridicality of religious experience. In defence of the psychological challenge, Leary's research corroborates the argument that religious experiences are illusory; he recorded the experiences of both LSD users and those who claimed to have had a religious experience, finding that the descriptions produced were almost indistinguishable from one another. Thus, the psychological challenge does have a case to make, since the influence of drugs on the mind denotes that all mind experiences are brain experiences, as the neuroscientist Persinger asserts.

A more full exploration of Persinger would be better, but this is a well-argued paragraph, or pair of paragraphs which are arguing the neurosis case.

Richard Swinburne (The Existence of God) made a ground – breaking contribution to the religious experience debate in his proposition of the two principles of credulity and testimony. The former essentially proposes that we have good reason to believe what we experience is true, insofar that our empiricist view of the world demands us to do so. This is a logical assertion to make, seeing as reliance on our senses has been instrumental to our functioning for centuries. Swinburne does however acknowledge that there is reason to discredit the experience if it is the product of hallucinogenic drugs such as LSD, or if the recipient was a devout atheist for example, as this would be a contradiction in terms. J.L Mackie however refutes religious experiences even if such experiences are produced in a state of sobriety; he argues that it is 'insufficiently critical' to do so as the experience allegedly lacks authority. A counter to this though is that a medium must exist through which God communicates the experience – if it is the mind, this doesn't necessarily dethrone the authority of the experience. Religious experiences surely have to be processed somewhere.

This is a good use of Swinburne. He is key to this debate and understanding the principles of credulity and testimony are paramount.

Nonetheless, Swinburne proposes the principle of testimony, which asserts that we should believe what we are told under the exception that the communicator of the knowledge is a renowned liar. William Alston's contribution also serves as support for Swinburne. Alston asserts that it is a 'double standard' to discredit religious experiences as like all others, they too are derived from sensory experience. Take a red car, for example: its colour is assumed to be validated by the unanimous testimony of all those who witness it and their judgement is formed empirically with the faculty of sight. Thus, Alston would argue that religious experiences are not illusory on his basis of belief that checking others' religious experiences validates them.

A good use of Alston to support Swinburne; though the term 'epistemic imperialism' would be a welcome addition.

To conclude, it could be argued that religious experiences are not illusory on the basis of Swinburne's approach to veridicality. Swinburne's assertion that not all have religious experiences because not all recognise them is highly plausible, especially when viewed in conjunction with his telephone analogy. Furthermore, Swinburne's thesis is convincing enough a more open – minded approach for 'psychological phenomena' for without proof, it is impossible to either fully reject or accept religious experiences as being unequivocally genuine.

Overall: A* [39/40]

The candidate's conclusion is non-committal, though, as the introduction suggests, it has critiqued religious experience so that we cannot accept them as given. It might have been better for the candidate to use James' evidence more in this essay and draw a stronger conclusion.

AO1: 16/16

The candidate has shown excellent comprehension of the demands of the question and has answered it throughout the essay. Further, the candidate has shown top quality knowledge and the use of supporting scholars demonstrates excellent understanding and the use of Teresa of Avila's experience is nuanced and complex. The candidate has used the material expertly in building the cases for and against.

AO2: 23/24

The candidate has shown an excellent ability to argue the cases for and against, and answer the question thoroughly and throughout the essay. Each position is analysed and evaluated with supporting and challenging scholars. Each position is developed and fully justified, with no views simply asserted. The line of reasoning is well developed and runs through the essay. The only way to improve it would be to draw a clear conclusion as to why the cases for and against are both so convincing. For example, considering the fact that so many people attest to religious experiences in James' research, it might show that at least the belief in these experiences is genuine and that Swinburne's principles prevent us from calling them all illusion in absence of evidence to the contrary.

'The problem of evil proves that there can be no God.' Discuss. (40/40 Grade A*)

The problem of evil is the most commonly used argument when challenge the existence of God, for which reason it is called the 'Rock of Atheism' according to Hans Kung. The argument seeks to undermine God by showing how God's classical attributes cannot be reconciled to the existence of evil and suffering, presented by Epicurus, Hume and more recently Mackie and McCloskey. God is defended by various theodicies, including Augustine's and Hick's variation of Irenaeus', however, it is a combination of this with a humble approach to our understanding of God that demonstrates that no challenge, even the problem of evil and suffering, can actually prove that God cannot exist.

This is a very strong opening making it clear what the essay is about and where the candidate will take it. There is reference to scholars supporting the challenge and defending God, so we expect to see them mentioned in the rest of the essay.

The Inconsistent Triad presented first by Epicurus and then again by David Hume posits that God is taken to be all loving and all powerful. If this was the case then God would have the power or the will to prevent it. So either God is not all loving or all powerful. McCloskey and Mackie further developed this argument in their logical problem of evil where they posited that God was all-loving, all-powerful, and all-knowing, so God should not only have the power and will to prevent evil, but also know of the evil and suffering that would come able and so all suffering is ultimately accountable to God.

This is a good, brief outline of the problem of evil in its two chief forms, the Inconsistent Triad and the Logical Problem of Evil. No time was wasted giving unnecessary details.

In response to these challenges, we find two main theodicies, the first presented by St Augustine and the second originally conceived by Irenaeus but developed by John Hick. Augustine's theodicy tried to respond to the challenge of the problem of evil by approaching it in this way: If God made all things and evil exist then God made evil, which is contradictory to the nature of God. In response to this challenge, he postulated, firstly, that God made everything and that, as asserted in the Bible, everything was made very good; this links to Gottfried Leibniz' assertion that this is the best of all possible worlds. Secondly, Augustine stated that evil is not a force itself but a privation of goodness. Therefore, God did not make evil, evil is the privation of the goodness that God made. This is supported by Herbert McCabe who stated that we know what grapes and deckchairs should be like and so we know when they go bad. Additionally, this marries perfectly with Plato's notion of how the Essential Form of Goodness, which Plotinus identified as God, shines through the FORMs and if an object is broken or bad it does not have that Goodness in it, and Aristotle's notion of purpose, if a thing is bad it is because it cannot fulfil its final cause. Thus, evil occurs when things do not live up to their expectations. Since God made everything to be good, it is us who spoil them. Therefore the harm we do to others is our responsibility, not God's. Though Augustine did not take the story of The Fall in Genesis as literal, the symbol of the story is apt, where we disobey God, we suffer.

This is a very developed, if long-winded, treatment of Augustine's theodicy. There is excellent use of examples and a nuanced connection with Plato and Aristotle which is not part of the syllabus, so it shows that the candidate understands the synoptic view of different scholars in their views of God's nature and relationship to good things. Synoptic points make wider linkages and will be credited..

As powerful as Augustine's theodicy is, it fails to adequately respond to the existence of natural evil and suffering such as that identified by more contemporary thinkers, including John Stuart Mill who argued that the extent to the suffering that appears in nature is so vast that there cannot possibly be a benevolent designer and Richard Dawkins who presented the example of the digger wasp which paralyses its victims in order to lay eggs inside them. In his debate with Douglas Wilson, Christopher Hitchens comments that the evils of human beings and the suffering we endure cannot be reconciled to any powerful and loving God, and that the belief in such a God is itself immoral. Augustine's solution is how angels themselves are responsible for natural evil as they are part of the hierarchy of creation. However, this is a very pre-scientific paradigm of the world which is not taken seriously by any rational scholar, religious or otherwise.

The contemporary examples given here are excellently chosen to emphasise how inadequate Augustine's theodicy is in dealing with natural suffering. There is another way to interpret Augustine's response to natural evil, that is, that through our disobedience of God it is we who see suffering as evil in nature; lions do not see natural suffering as evil, but as part of nature. The candidate has made a similar case later. Wise not to over develop Augustine as the essay is not specifically asking about Augustine's theodicy.

Hick's variation of Irenaeus' theodicy gives us some more hope. His theodicy argues that we are created in God's image, but not His likeness. We are born in an embryonic state and that life is a journey of soul-making to be more like God. If the world contained no suffering and we were just good because we were made to be good, then there would be no value in life and no value in our goodness. Like Alvin Plantinga argues in the Free Will defence, God cannot make us good as we would be robots and not freely good agents. The same applies to natural suffering. Peter Vardy identified five types of natural suffering: animal suffering, mental illness, natural disasters, frailty of the human body and diseases. So, according to Hick, without all this suffering, there is no way we can strive to better ourselves, serve each other and be more like Christ who is the perfect Man. Thus, suffering is necessary and, as Gottfried

Leibniz asserted, this is the best of all possible worlds, even with suffering in it. There is no other way the world could have been made.

This is a good treatment of Hick, soul-making and a good link to Plantinga. This responds to the problem of natural suffering which Augustine's theodicy failed to do convincingly.

Suffice it to say, many atheists and even theists do not accept this as a solution as it would suggest that an all-powerful God could not create a world where we could be good and not have to suffer to such a great extent. Additionally, it makes God even more malignant. Stephen Fry echoes David Attenborough's comment that the God who put the whale in the ocean put the parasite in the eye of an impoverished child. This is no loving God, but a cruel one, one that Fry calls a 'maniac'.

This is a good link back to the problem, now citing the omniscience attribute as the reason why Hick's theodicy is unfair. Again, the candidate uses contemporary scholars and thinkers very well.

In resolution to the weight of the problem, there is another response. Firstly, the Inconsistent Triad is actually undermined by the Logical Problem of Evil. The former identifies how evil cannot exist if God is benevolent and omnipotent, but the latter states God cannot be omnipotent, benevolent and omniscient, as though suddenly God could be omnipotent and benevolent and there be evil, if he was not aware of it. Thus, perhaps we are so ignorant of what God actually is, that were we to know it even the Logical Problem of Evil would be undermined itself. As Lady Philosophy asserts to Boethius, the problem is with human understanding not the nature of God.

This is a clever insight into the contradiction between the two problems of evil. This is rarely noticed. The link to Lady Philosophy is nuanced and insightful.

Secondly, the problem with the problem of evil and suffering is the very equating of evil with suffering. It is a Benthamite notion that pleasure equates to good and pain equates to bad/evil. There is no rational reason why we should make that connection. We can accept that we dislike pain and like pleasure, but pleasure can lead to bad ends (overdosing on drugs, tooth decay) and goodness can come from pain (birth, exam success after lots of revision), so the very argument itself is based on a category error. There is no problem of evil and suffering, as evil and suffering are not the same things. Evil is the absence of good, and suffering is a thing that happens in the world God created.

Again, this is a very clever insight into the correlation between evil and suffering. The link to Bentham is clever as the connection between evil and suffering is one of pleasure/pain equating to good/bad. To call the problem of evil and suffering a category error is very insightful.

In conclusion, the proponents for the challenge argue that God cannot exist as there is too much suffering in the world among humans and in the natural world and that this is irreconcilable with God's existence. Hume presented the Inconsistent Triad and McCloskey and Mackie presented the Logical Problem of Evil. In response to these and other challenges, Augustine argued that suffering was man made and that we were accountable, at least for moral evil, and Hick argued suffering is necessary for our soul-making. However, the most convincing defence is that it is a category error to consider evil and suffering as the same thing. Suffering is something that happens and evil is the rational decision to deprive goodness from others. Thus God, whose nature we cannot possibly know and comprehend, allows suffering for His own omniscient reasons.

This is an excellent conclusion, summing up the case for and the case against, reiterating the theodicies and the final resolution.

Overall 40/40 Grade A*

AO1 16/16

The candidate has shown excellent knowledge and understanding of the question, has used a variety of scholarly opinions, outline the problem of evil in various ways, presented both theodicies on the syllabus and given a third alternative bridging the gap between. The essay is packed with nuanced knowledge, examples and connections between the scholars and views.

AO2 24/24

The candidate has shown an excellent capability to analyse and evaluate the essay. Each position is challenged, the theodicies are analysed, weaknesses are found in all places and an excellent variety of scholarly views are used to defend all positions and challenge them again. The candidate has shown great insights into the problem of evil and the workings of the theodicies themselves.

Critically assess the philosophical problems raised by the belief that God is omnipotent. (33/40 Grade A)

The question of God's omnipotence has been debated throughout time, in the Bible and by contemporary scholars. Rather that this rather generic opening part of the sentence, the candidate might have made more of the fact that God's omnipotence is discussed across various disciplines: 'The nature of God as being omnipotent has been discussed and debated across biblical study, philosophy and theology.' The problem of evil suggests that an omnipotent God can't exist whilst on the other hand, Augustine and Irenaeus' theodicies prove that suffering in the world doesn't undermine the notion of an all-powerful God.

It is good that the candidate has chosen to identity the problem of evil as part of the overall problem of God's omnipotence, but this is not in itself the most pressing philosophical question related to God's omnipotence, the most being: What does it mean to call God omnipotent? Additionally, there should be a thesis statement that will direct this essay.

It is important, first, to establish what God's omnipotence means. Kenny argues that God's omnipotence is firstly found in theophany events in the Bible, such as the creation of the world and the miracle of God granting Joshua to stop the sun - God has power over nature. This is a good way to start this paragraph, identifying that we must first establish what omnipotence means and look firstly at biblical accounts. Kenny's name was unnecessary here. Descartes argues that it means that God can do the logically impossible. Since God as created the axioms of the earth he must obey his own rules of history, logic and maths not ours, so God can do what is logically impossible for us, for example, making, what appears to us to be, square circles etc. *This is an excellent and direct treatment of Descartes' definition of omnipotence.* Anselm asserts that God is 'that than which nothing greater can be conceived' which means that he can't lose control of his actions as this would contradict his omnipotence. *Good, another interesting development on what should be able to do. It should be noted that this contradicts Descartes' definition.* Additionally, God is what Aristotle calls the unmoved mover, uncaused cause, pure necessity and actuality. This is further developed by Aquinas' assertion that God can do whatever it is logical for God to do, thus contradicting Descartes' definition. Therefore, this is what it means to call God omnipotent.

A good paragraph, though it might have been worthwhile putting the philosophical approaches more chronologically and showing a comparison. Strange that the concluding sentence asserts 'this is what it means to call God omnipotent' when there are two contradicting views that are unresolved: God omnipotence is unlimited and God's omnipotence is limited.

God's omnipotence can be challenged however. Hume questions whether if God was all powerful, how is there suffering in the world? Kant would argue that suffering can't be universalised and so can't be moral. If God is the source of morality, how can he be omnipotent on one hand and allow suffering on the other hand as pointed out in Mackie and McCloskey's Logical Problem of Evil. Examples of suffering in the world stem from propositional truths in the Bible such as Adam and Eve's sin through the modern day in evil such as terrorism and natural disasters that human can't control - natural evil pointed out by Mill. Therefore, the problem of evil suggests God can't be omnipotent.

A good and brief treatment of the problem of evil and how it is raised by God's supposed omnipotence.

However, this argument can be rebutted. Firstly, Augustine's Theodicy suggests that the reason for evil in the world is human free will and reason which is 'fallen' according to Barth. An omnipotent God is what Plato calls the 'Essential Form of Goodness', supported by what Plotinus calls God as 'goodness, life and beauty'. Similarly, the Augustine Theodicy supports that it is human privation that causes evil and a misuse of free will. This suggests that the problem of evil doesn't undermine God's omnipotence. Similarly, it's humans that associate suffering with evil. Good doesn't necessarily equal pain. McCabe's example of broken deckchairs can be used - just because something doesn't meet our expectation doesn't mean it's bad. Our free will causes the actions we take and therefore the consequences - this is supported in how CS Lewis states that the 'door to hell is locked from the inside'. God can still be therefore deemed omnipotent despite pain.

This is a good direct response using the theodicies and attitudes to hell to justify God in the face of suffering.

God's omnipotence can also be challenged from a miracle point of view. An example of a miracle from the Bible is Jairus' daughter in St Mark's gospel. If God is all powerful, why doesn't he perform a miracle like this on everyone? Maurice Wiles, who is supported by Pseudo-Dionysius, suggests that God actually can't perform miracles as it defies his own laws such as logic. *How does pseudo-Dionysius support Wiles?* This notion puts restrictions on God' power. However, if as Anselm suggests, God is greater that what we can understand, God not performing miracles on all of us may be part of our telos as Aristotle suggests even if we can't comprehend that. Also beyond our comprehension is the afterlife. Just because God doesn't grant us a miracle doesn't mean he isn't omnipotent, we may be rewarded with entry into heaven, a Thomist view. The concept of miracles doesn't therefore entirely undermine God's omnipotence.

A nice nuanced approach since 'Miracles' is no longer on the syllabus. The candidate has clearly done additional research to form another argument to challenge and defend God's omnipotence. It might have been nice to add Gottfried Leibniz to support Anselm: If this is the 'best of all possible worlds' then God literally could not perform more miracles or stop suffering etc.

In conclusion, the problem of suffering doesn't undermine God's omnipotence. We can't ever fully understand God's plan and it is humans who have decided that suffering is bad rather than viewing it as necessary. Human free will that God has granted us as a creator, not a dictator means suffering isn't something that can be entirely blamed on God. God isn't the 'maniac' Fry paints him as.

It is always unwise to put new quotes and arguments in a conclusion. If the 'maniac' God was a point that the candidate wanted to challenge, then it should really have been raised in the introduction and then the candidate should have stated that the essay would disprove this assertion.

Overall 33/40, Grade A

AO1: 14/16

The candidate has shown excellent knowledge and understanding of the overall topic. There is clear nuanced knowledge looking at miracles and the various aspects of the problem of evil, including the inconsistent triad and the logical problem of evil, as well as looking at the various interpretations of God's knowledge. That candidate uses excellent language and has given a library of scholarly views. The candidate clearly knows the material. The only thing that should have been further developed is Aquinas' assertion that God can do only what is logical for God to do, and how this contradicts Descartes' view.

AO2: 19/24

The analysis and evaluation is very good as the question has been answered directly and appropriately throughout the essay. The candidate should have focused the essay on the definitions of God, rather than the problem of evil, however, the essay was not unbalanced towards the problem of evil. It is always important to know what the question is asking - its underlying agenda. In this case it is the philosophical problems raised by God's omnipotence, the first being, what does it mean? There is a very good use of evaluating scholarly views, the knowledge is very good, some additional insights would have been good to see, for example, the way that Mackie's logical problem of evil (providing three attributes for God) undermines the challenge presented by the inconsistent triad (which provides only two attributes for God),. This begs the question 'would the challenge presented by the logical problem of evil be undermined if we knew another attributed for God?' Additionally, going on from the omission of the development of Aquinas and Descartes, a good insight would have been how both Aquinas' and Descartes' views of God are not mutually exclusive: God can do the illogical (from our perspective) which remaining logical (from his perspective).

Critically assess the traditional Christian concept of God being eternal. (40/40 Grade A*)

The word 'eternal' has been defined in numerous different ways by theist, agnostic and atheist philosophers. One such definition is that for an object or being to be eternal, it must have a beginning but never end (unless time itself also ends) – an object such as this exists within time and will continue to exist until time itself no longer exists. However, this definition is largely regarded as 'ever-lasting' as opposed to eternal. Another definition of eternal then, is an object which, although existing within time, has no beginning or end. This definition is similar to the previous with one vital difference: the object does not have a moment of conception; its existence is inextricably linked to time and, for as long as time exists, so too will this object exist (yet the object still does exist within time). The final definition, however, contradicts both of the previous definitions and states that, in order for an object or being to be eternal, it must exist entirely outside of time. This is the definition upon which Christianity traditionally places its belief of God as eternal and, as a result of this fact, will be the definition discussed in this essay.

This is an excellent introduction, in that the candidate has defined both interpretations of the term 'eternal' which is the attribute of God being evaluated here. The candidate has distinguished between the two variations of eternal: everlastingness and timelessness (though the latter term here is not used). This shows us that the candidate will be exploring how these terms have been assigned to the nature of God.

This definition of eternity in relation to God was put forward by Boethius in his Consolation of Philosophy (524) and, since shortly after the books' creation, has been regarded as the traditional view of God's existence in relation to time; indeed, Aquinas supported this view in his Summa Theologica, thereby further cementing it in the Christian tradition. *This is excellent background to the Boethius contribution shown the relationship between Boethius' work and that of Augustine.* The view was initially put forward by Boethius as an attempt to explain how humans could retain their free-will with an omniscient God who could see every human's future: he reached the conclusion that God must not exist within the time-frame which all of humanity does.

This is subtly done which is very good; the candidate has not wasted time going into the details of Boethius' dilemma as it is not relevant to this question, though the nature of that dilemma is mentioned as being the birth of this theory.

While God may know of our future, it is not the future for him as he does not exist within time. In this definition, God has no concept of time and exists in a continuous present with no concept of future or past; he sees all of human history in a simultaneous instant. Boethius himself explains this by stating that God has the 'simultaneous and perfect possession of boundless life.' While this theory may be strong and explained eloquently by Boethius, it has come under severe criticism by innumerable philosophers (particularly in the last century), both religious and atheistic including Richard Swinburne, Kenny and Brian Davies.

A lovely summative paragraph bringing together Boethius' understanding of God's eternity. Note that the candidate has correctly presented this as Boethius' contribution, though in 'Consolations of Philosophy' it is Lady Philosophy who reveals it to Boethius. When answering a question where you are required to distinguish between Boethius' dilemma, human freewill and rewards/punishments, and the solution to the dilemma, God's eternity, be clear about which voice you are detailing from 'Consolations': Boethius' and Lady Philosophy's.

This being said, the traditional Christian view of God's eternity has a number of great strengths. Perhaps the greatest strength of the theory is put forward by St. Thomas Aquinas. He claims that, in the human world, change and time are blatantly inextricably linked: humans grow old and die, buildings erode and collapse, metal rusts and memories are forgotten. If God were to exist within time and be constrained by the same laws which time inflicts upon the universe, he too would be susceptible to change. *The candidate is nicely linking God's eternity to the other attributes of God, in this case immutability.* However, both the bible and Christian tradition state that God is ineffable and cannot change (in Malachi 3:6 it states that 'I the Lord do not change.'). *Great use of scripture here; be sure to have a bank of passages you can call upon. Do not worry about accurate quotes, paraphrasing is perfectly acceptable.* Indeed, the ability to or even the possibility to undergo change seems to imply imperfection; a perfect being would have no need to change seeing as any change would be detrimental. Surely a God who ages, forgets or deteriorates in any way would not be worthy of worship. Clearly then, owing to the fact that God is perfect and the fact that he doesn't change, he must not exist within time. *The candidate justified this assertion well.* However, despite the strength of this point, it has come under criticism, namely by Christian philosophers who believe that God is in fact capable of change. In the bible, God is shown to forge a covenant with the Israelites; he speaks of his love for them (as well as all mankind), asks them to perform tasks and gave them the Ten Commandments. Clearly, as is evident from human experience, it is impossible to take part in a relationship of any kind without it altering your way of life at least to a minute degree. Surely then, if God did indeed enter into a covenant with the Israelites, it must have altered him at least in some way, particularly if he loved them as is stated in the bible. Moreover, God is frequently referred to as having human-like emotions towards the people with which he creates relationships including surprise (Isiah 5). Surely if God can be surprised, he is susceptible to change and, as a result of this the traditional view that God must exist outside of time owing to the fact that he cannot change may be fundamentally flawed.

Moreover, not only does God's ineffable nature cause problems with the traditional view of God's eternity when examples of relationships between God and humans are brought into question, but the very fact that God is able to form these relationships in the first place seems to contradict the traditional Christian view of God's eternal nature. Indeed, if Boethius' theory is to be accepted as the traditional Christian view, it seems to contradict any instances where God enters the human time-frame to intervene directly, whether that be through the answering of prayers, miracles or the coming of Jesus. *The candidate has brought the problem to the fore by bringing the argument to the problem of miracles.* According to the traditional view of God's eternity, he has no concept of past, present, future or universal time in general. Instead, Boethius and Aquinas would argue, he exists outside of time and sees all of humanities actions throughout all of time in a simultaneous, instantaneous present. If this were the case, it would surely be impossible for God to pick a particular time in history and intervene directly because God has no concept of human time. For example, according to Christianity, God directly intervened in the life of Mary and made her pregnant with Jesus, his son. This intervention from God on a specific date in history would arguably be impossible for a God who has absolutely no concept of time.

This is perhaps a slight misunderstanding of the notion of timelessness. It is not that God has 'no notion of time' it is more that 'God is not subject to time'. Boethius' presentation of God's eternity is one where God sees all of time laid out before him, like the many slides of a movie. In this way, one could theorise, God could do exactly what the candidate has dismissed; He could pick a slide and jump in, like Mary Poppins jumping into the chalk drawing.

This criticism, therefore, has a very damaging implication. If the traditional view of God's eternity is kept then it would be impossible for any events throughout history where God directly intervened to be true (including the coming of Jesus). Owing to the fact that the vast majority of Christians would disagree with this statement, it seems likely that the traditional view of God's eternal nature demanding he be outside of time would be regarded as incorrect by most.

The candidate has reasoned this point, albeit with some errors, which shows an attempt at justification. It is a good attempt to evaluate the involvement of God in the world, but perhaps the use of Wiles would be better to show that God could not be involved in the world as it would challenge his overall benevolence given that he picks and chooses where and when to be involved, e.g. in ancient Egypt and not in Auschwitz.

That being said, however, it is possible for a Christian believer to retain his/her belief in the traditional view of God's eternity while still believing in direct intervention from God owing to a very simple explanation. While it may seem to be an impossibility for God to exist outside of time and manage to affect events within time, it is entirely possible that human's merely lack the mental capacity to fully understand God's nature and the way in which he acts. As an omnipotent being, it may be entirely possible for God to exist outside of time yet still will events to happen within our human universe. Indeed, Aquinas' theory of Eternal Law states that God's nature is only knowable through simplistic reflections and that the true complexity and power of God's true nature cannot be comprehended by us as humans.

A lovely evaluation of human feebleness.

The candidate could have drawn upon Boethius once more with the theory of knowledge and how knowledge of an object is relative to the subjective nature of the knower of the object.

However, this is not a particularly strong point because, as Aquinas and C.S. Lewis state, and as is generally accepted by Christians, although God is all-powerful, he can still not perform actions which are logically impossible. Descartes disagreed with this and stated that God could do anything, whether logically possible or not. It would seem to many that being able to exist both within and outside of time is a logical impossibility and, as a result, cannot be done even by God. Therefore, I would argue that this point further weakens the traditional view of God's eternal nature.

The candidate has used multiple scholarly opinions to evaluate this point about what is logically possible for God to do. It would be worth considering Descartes' position a little further. Descartes said that God can do the logically possible and impossible; typical responses would err towards Aquinas' notion that God cannot do what is logically impossible; this would defend God from challenges such as can God create a stone he cannot lift etc.

However, upon reflection, Descartes' point holds some value: our understanding of logic and mathematics work insofar as we understand them and God wills them to work. Taking a point made by Keith Ward, if we can know the universe it is because God has known it into existence; therefore what we know is what God allows us to know. Theoretically, therefore, what we consider logical is what God has allowed us to know to be logical. God could therefore have known into being what we consider illogical, thus Descartes is right. Ultimately, God created logic, so He can do what he wants.

A further, similar weakness of the traditional view of God's eternity is put forward by both Richard Swinburne and Anthony Kenny (both of whom are Christians). This weakness is similar to the previous as it is also concerned with the impossibility of acts which are logically impossible to achieve. Both philosophers argued that Boethius' idea of God seeing and knowing everything from outside of time in a simultaneous present is incoherent. Kenny attempts to highlight the ridiculousness of this theory by stating that, according to this view of God's eternal nature, 'The great fire of Rome is simultaneous with the whole of eternity.' Swinburne further supported this point and practically dismissed the entire theory by claiming that it 'doesn't make much sense.' *The candidate could have afforded Swinburne a little more development here: Swinburne argues that God cannot know what it is like to be in 1995 unless He was in fact in 1995, in which case God must be in time.* It should be noted that both Swinburne and Kenny seem to be leaning towards a belief in God as ever-lasting as opposed to eternal in a Boethian sense. *This is a satisfactory assessment of the Kenny/Swinburne challenge.* However, this criticism is extremely weak. Neither Boethius nor Aquinas claimed that all of time takes place at once; indeed, if this was the case it would be incorrect. Boethius instead claimed that the nature of God's knowledge is so different to humans' that he, as an omniscient being, sees all of eternity in a simultaneous present. The nature of knowledge which God possesses isn't constricted by time and, as a result of this, God is able to take in all the knowledge of the universe simultaneously; the events do not actually happen simultaneously. Indeed, Paul Helm puts this criticism succinctly and claims that 'God, considered as timeless, cannot have temporal relations with any of his creation. He is timeless in the sense of being time free.' He then goes on to accuse Kenny and Swinburne of reduction ad absurdum (over-simplifying the argument to ridiculous degrees to try and prove it as incorrect). For this reason, I would argue that Kenny and Swinburne's criticism doesn't weaken the traditional theory of God's eternal nature at all.

This is an excellent evaluation of the challenge using Paul Helm including some good quotations and technical language. Some of these paragraphs are rather long.

A strength of the traditional Christian view of God's eternal nature which is also routed in God's separation from the time-bound universe is put forward by

Anselm and has been elaborated on innumerable philosophers. The essence of Anselm's argument is that, as a perfect being, God cannot be contained or restricted by anything. For this reason, Anselm would argue, not even time or the universe could contain him, thereby making it illogical for God to be within time as Swinburne and Kenny would argue. *A good reading of Anselm here.* This point can be further supported with reference to God's creation of the universe. Logically, it seems impossible for any being (God included) to create a reality and then exist within it; God must have existed outside of the universe prior to its creation in order for him to have created it. *A simple example would be for a builder to exist within his creation.* Moreover, seeing as time is a feature of the universe, it seems likely that God would not be affected by it if he is not a part of our physical universe. While philosophers such as Descartes would argue that it is possible for even God to act in such a way as is logically impossible, I would argue that this is a fairly clear strength of the traditional view of God's eternal nature.

Another good evaluation of the challenge.

However, many have argued that Boethius' entire theory of God's eternal nature relies too heavily on the influence of Platonic and Aristotelian philosophy and isn't actually based in Christian knowledge. Indeed, the idea of a God who exists in a separate reality from humans seems to be a Christianised reflection of Aristotle's idea of a Prime Mover God and his perfect, ineffability seems to draw from Plato's idea of the perfect, unchanging realm of the forms. *This observation is not without merit; the classical understanding of God is based in Biblical Revelation as well as Greek philosophy.* However, I would argue that this criticism is extremely weak. Just because Boethius adapted some of his ideas from the ancient Greek philosophers doesn't mean that his theory isn't applicable to the Christian faith. Indeed, the mere fact that St. Thomas Aquinas supported the theory combined with the fact that it has been accepted as the general, traditional view of God's eternity seems to prove that, despite its roots in Pagan philosophy, it is entirely applicable to Christianity. *Let us not forget that Aquinas translated the works of Aristotle into Latin and developed his ideas from Aristotle.* Certainly, Christianity as a faith itself is largely based on ancient Greek Philosophy. For this reason, the traditional Christian view on the eternal nature of God is not weakened by its Platonic and Aristotelian roots.

Well justified.

Overall, therefore, I believe it is clear that Boethius' theory of the eternity of God as is put forward in his Consolation of Philosophy, which has been agreed with by Thomas Aquinas and generally accepted as the traditional Christian view is a strong, well thought out theory. However, despite this, I believe that this theory's apparent inability to support the view that God can interact with the universe, affect people directly and intervene at specific points in time weaken it significantly. Clearly, a huge percentage of Christians believe that God has the ability to affect what happens in our universe and, if the traditional view is to be accepted, it seems unlikely that this could be true. Therefore, I would argue that the fact that the traditional view of God's eternal nature seems to disagree with the traditional view of God's actions within the universe cause the theory to be far from perfect.

Overall: A * [40/40]

The candidate has summed up the case for God's eternity and the case challenging it. The candidate has shown that there are benefits but that many of the challenges weaken the perspective. It would have been refreshing for the candidate to conclude with a more fixed point of view, for example, one where God is both eternal AND everlasting as Christian theology actually maintains, hence the understanding of the Triune God of scripture: the Father is eternal, the Holy Spirit is everlasting within the universe and the Son walked as a man and is present in the world in the tabernacle. This would have shown a real understanding of the Christian notion of how God's eternity can be reconciled with the challenges of Swinburne and modern miracle-maintaining Christians.

AO1: 16/16

The candidate has assessed the traditional nature of God's eternity well and consistently throughout the essay, calling upon scholarly ideas throughout. Each paragraph has been used to deal with a separate aspect of God's eternity, from the challenges posed by Boethius' 'Consolations' to the Cartesian notion of God's ability to act illogically. Each challenge has been dealt with directly and in a sophisticated manner. The candidate could have explored the notion of God's everlasting eternity more calling upon his revelation throughout in scripture and the need for an imminent God for the existence of miracles to work. The candidate has shown an excellent variety of knowledge calling upon scholars both in and outside of the taught syllabus, giving quotes, key names and varied arguments. The candidate's understanding is evident in the appropriate application of each scholar and theory in order to assess of God's eternity. The candidate has selected elements of both classical and contemporary scholars and even synoptically linked to Greek philosophy. Finally, key language and terms were used appropriately and to a sophisticated level.

AO2: 24/24

The candidate fully engaged with the question as evidenced by the fluidity of the paragraphs covering a full range of challenges to God's eternity and the assessment of various responses to those challenges; the candidate ensured that the engagement was evident as the end of each paragraph was linked back to the question. Material beyond the taught syllabus for this topic was used, including Plato and Aristotle as well as the assessment of God's ability to do the logical and illogical. All concepts were analysed fully; there were the odd assertion that was incorrect or incomplete, however, this was the exception and due to positive marking, this would not lower the candidate's overall mark. Finally, the essay was fully evaluative as the candidate assessed varied aspects of the topic, analysing each and drawing conclusions.

"Symbols are the only meaningful way of talking about God.' Discuss. (38/40 Grade A*)

"A symbol" in general is something that stands, or it is used in place of some other thing. Paul Tillich for instance, believed that symbolic language can be the only meaningful way on God-Talk, because "it opens up levels of reality which otherwise were closed to us". *This is a good use of Paul Tillich early on; since the question is asking about symbols it is important to open with Paul Tillich who is on the syllabus to demonstrate that you are addressing the question directly.* Symbols are not the only way on talking about God, Moses Maimonides identified negative language can bring us closer to understand God, or even by analogies as Aquinas says "they bring us" into ultimate concern- to understand that God is unknowable to us. So in some extent, symbols are the only meaningful way on talking about God.

The candidate has presented both sides of the debate: the case for using symbols as presented by Tillich and the case for using other methods of God-talk, the examples given being Via Negativa as presented by Moses Maimonides and Analogy as presented by Aquinas. The candidate has also added a hint as to the thesis of the essay. It is there though it could have been made more evidence that this is in fact the thesis statement.

Tillich started his point by saying that the meaning of the words when used symbolically is always "partially negated by that which they point". For example, when we are claiming "God is our father" we are negating the meaning of the word father in a biological/human sense, and opening up a deeper meaningful way in God-talk because as Leibniz says God is beyond to human comprehension. *This is an excellent explanation of Tillich's interpretation of symbols and a good link to Leibniz.* This is similar to via Negativa, according to Maimonides "you will come nearer to the knowledge and comprehension of God by the negative attributes." The same it is with symbols, when we use symbolical language in God-talk we come closer to comprehension of God because symbols represent something beyond our direct experience.

The candidate is making interesting comparisons between the use of symbols and the use of Via Negativa. This is showing that the candidate understands the uses of these methods of God-talk and the extent to which they bring us to an understanding of God.

However, Macquarie believed that symbolic language is a language of mind, because it "bounces off" the subject of the speaker on what wishes to refer. To clarify this point we might refer to R.M. Hare idea of blik, everyone owns a blik - which is a way that individual interprets the world. So symbols can be ambiguous because people by using symbolic language can bring their own interpretation of God. Therefore, symbols are not a clearly meaningful way in God-talk as it leads us into a subjective interpretation. *Great link to Hare's bliks here; this is a clever way of outlining the challenges raised by relying on subjective symbols.* Furthermore, in religious language not all is symbolic, when Christians talk about Jesus' Resurrection, they do not mean it symbolically, but they actually hold a literal meaning for that empirical event. So as Wittgenstein might argue it depends on the context, "symbols" might be a meaningless way on talking about God into literal meaning, but into a symbolic context might be meaningful as they make sense within the context.

The candidate has raised an important issue here; in the same way that Flew challenges defenders of God-talk against falsification claiming that believers do in fact mean that Jesus' resurrection is a scientific fact, the candidate has shown that symbols needs a context within which to make sense. It would have been better if the candidate had made the falsification link when stating that "not all is symbolic".

Also, most ignore the fact that symbols grow out of the individual or collective unconscious and cannot function without being accepted from everybody. This can be counted as a meaningful way on talking about God, because symbols are not only involved within the mind, but are recognisable from everyone. *This is an interesting spin on the challenge presented that symbols are subjective; the candidate is arguing that symbols have are intrinsically social. A link to Wittgenstein's Language Games would have been beneficial here.* This in a way recalls what Kant says about universalisation of the maxim – if something is capable to be universalised then it can be considered as absolute. *A very interesting synoptic link to Kantian ethics.* Symbols can act the same, only if they are accepted by everybody, so they can be the only meaningful way on talking about God, as they are universal and cannot be invented.

The candidate has taken the challenge of the subjectivism of symbols and turned it around. This really needs Wittgenstein to pull together.

However, although symbols grow when the situation is ripe for them, they die out when the situation changes. So then change can act negatively on the way we talk about God. When symbols no longer produce a response in the group where they originally found expression, they then cannot be considered as a meaningful way on talking about God.

This is a reasoned assertion growing out of the previous paragraph which brings us back to the problem with symbols; being based in interpretation and social agreement, they do not last, unlike objective language. This latter point could have been explicitly stated.

Therefore, we can use analogy as a better meaningful way on talking about God, Aquinas in "analogia entis" (analogy of being) suggests that we can understand God through his creation – he can be known thought his objects and relationship of the natural order. This is analogy of attribution which is causal – we can understand the agent by looking at the product. So, analogy can be considered as a more meaningful way on talking about God than symbols, because symbols do suggest that to know God, while in Aquinas' idea of analogy do not attempt to know God, rather it recognises that there is a higher being and help us to realise that we do not know God – "to know God is to know him". For example, by using analogy of proportion concerning in God-talk we comprehend that everything within the physical world fulfils their expectations, while "God's expectation is to be infinitely greater than us".

This is a lovely use of analogy as a comparison to symbols as an effective way of talking about God. The candidate's point about how symbols require a knowledge of God, unlike analogy which accepts that we cannot know God is especially insightful.

As Macquarie argues symbolic language is the language of the mind, therefore it can be easily mislead down to subjectivism, this is why analogy is a better meaningful way in God-talk, because by using analogical language we observe the word empirically and consequently deduce that there must be a higher being above, we just incapable to understand his nature.

The candidate has used Macquarie well here, though it would have been beneficial to mention the different types of symbols that Macquarie describes: conventional and intrinsic.

Concluding, in a way symbols are a meaningful way on talking about God as they opens up levels of reality, but they can be considered too personal when we try to interpret. However, it should not be ignored that they function within collective unconscious group, so symbols to be considered as meaningful must be accepted by a group, so they are not too personal or subjective because they unlock the direct dimension and go beyond. Ultimately, as Aquinas says God's expectation is to be infinitely greater than us, symbols in some extent equally bring us into this as analogy, because using symbolic language we try to reach a level of reality which cannot be reached in any other way.

Overall: A* [38/40]

The candidate has chosen to compare symbol and analogy in the conclusion to show how while symbolic language has its uses, its best use in order to reach a useful method of talking about God is through its adaptation into analogy. A well justified conclusion.

AO1: 14/16

The essay was introduced well and each paragraph dealt with a separate element of the topic. Where some candidates might have been put off by the narrowness of the question, asking about symbols, this candidate realised immediately, and showed this in the introduction, that the essay was asking for a comparison between symbolic language and other types of language. Note, that while the candidate used Hare's bliks and Language Games, the candidate did not mistake this essay question for one that was asking about the meaningfulness of God-talk, notice that there was no mention of Verificatonism etc. The candidate used a wide variety of knowledge, drawing upon symbols, Via Negativa, analogy and even challenges of falsification in order to evaluate this statement. The intelligent way that the candidate compared and linked arguments and scholars together demonstrates a sophisticated level of understanding of the concepts. The candidate chose well from the pool of knowledge, however, it would have been to the benefit of the essay if there were some stronger links to Wittgenstein's Language Games which seemed to be the way that the candidate was going, and Via Negativa was hardly used though it was mentioned in the introduction. Finally, terms were used accurately; the only criticism here would be that the candidate should have specified Tillich's distinction between symbols and signs and if Macquarie was to be used then also between conventional and intrinsic symbols.

AO2: 24/24

The candidate was fully engaged with the question from the outset which was evident though the way the introduction was formed, and the means by which each paragraph analysed and challenged the terms and concepts. There was a wide selection of material used and synoptic links were present throughout the essay demonstrating a sophisticated level of analysis. Assertions were never made without justification and criticism which demonstrates a highly analytic approach. Finally, various perspectives were evaluated which drew the ultimate conclusion.

'The Falsification Principle presents no real challenge to religious belief.' Discuss. (38/40 Grade A*)

If something is falsifiable, it is able to face scientific scrutiny based on the use of empirical evidence in order to justify or disprove its veridicalness. In the view of Vienna Circle-era philosophers, this is key to demarcating between scientific ideas from non-scientific ones. Flew even goes so far to say that talk about religion (God-Talk) is meaningless because it cannot be falsified. However, this challenge need not impact upon religious belief according to other philosophers such as John Wisdom, who say that the sole use of science as the judge of validity is fallacious as God does not fall into that category.

This is an excellent opening paragraph as it defines the terms being discussed and presents the two opposing sides to the debate, that which claims that God-talk is meaningless and that defends the use of God-talk on the basis that faith does not fall into the category of scientific endeavour, and so is not affected by it.

Karl Popper, a key falsificationist, said that falsification involves the demarcation between statements of science and statements of other things. This in itself shows that falsification need not challenge religious belief, because religious statements are simply not part of scientific study – they are Gould's idea of non-overlapping magisteria. *The candidate has made a good synoptic link it to Gould's 'non-overlapping magisteria' which is excellent.* Therefore, because falsification does not disprove God-Talk, but simply categorises it separately to statements of science, it presents no real challenge to religious belief. However, Anthony Flew went further than this to say that because God-Talk is unfalsifiable, it is actually meaningless because he takes the view that truth can only be found in empirically sense-observed statements.

Therefore, the falsification principle does present issues for God-Talk and religious belief.

It is very important to distinguish, as this candidate is doing, between Popper's falsificationism which is demarcation between scientific statements and other statements, and Flew's falsificationism which calls unfalsifiable statements meaningless. The candidate has made that distinction early on.

Flew's view could, on the other hand, be labelled as "epistemic imperialism" (an idea of Alston's) *Nicely added* – the rejection of all other methods of reading the truth in favour of one, and going on a "crusade" to endorse it. We can see this problem with the early astrologers, who rejected counter evidence for their own evidence because they did not like it. This epistemic imperialism can be accounted for by Hare's "blik" theory. This is that every person has their own personal "spin" on their worldview – a blik – that is not falsifiable and cannot be tested at all. Any conflict between people's bliks cannot be solved using reason due to their nature. As a result, Flew's and all falsificationists' ideas are a product of their bliks and so hold no real authority over any other blik, say, one of a deeply religious person, and so no challenge is provided to believers by the ideas of falsification. *The candidate has moved from Alston's challenge of Flew's epistemic imperialism and used it as a platform into Hare's bliks; this is a good transition and the candidate has used Hare to defend God-talk in the face of falsification very decisively.* On the other hand, Flew would respond possibly by saying that Christians do not see their beliefs as simply a blik, but as an assertion – something that can be falsified, for example "God created the universe". *Good point often missed by candidates.* This is wrong in itself due to the unfalsifiability of claims like this, and so falsification does challenge religious belief. *The candidate has successfully brought the problem right back even after the successful evaluation using Hare. Notice that the candidate is constantly and systematically bringing each paragraph back to the question. This is key to a Level 6 essay.*

Wittgenstein's "Language Games" theory applies very usefully here. This is the idea that when people talk about something, in this case God-Talk, they are taking part in a "game", where the words and syntax used take on a meaning that makes sense in that particular filed, but may not in other fields, for example the rules of chess would not apply in a game of football. *This is simply described with an example that makes it clear what the candidate is saying without droning on for paragraphs; to show additional nuanced knowledge the candidate might have used Wittgenstein's' own example of builders and blocks.* In a similar way as bliks, falsificationists are taking part in the language game of science, which while useful and relevant in itself, does not hold any authority over language games of other things, including religious belief and God-Talk. *The candidate is comparing bliks to Language Games which is a good comparison so long as it is made clear that bliks are personal or shared views of the world and Language Games are, by their nature, universal linguistic paradigms.* So, falsification poses no real threat to religious belief in this sense. As Wisdom says, God is outside of our human understanding – the language game of people – so should not be scrutinised in this way. *A good use of Wisdom to defend Wittgenstein and Hare.* We are not reliable enough to say we know enough about anything to do with God, similar to Kant's idea that we are limited by the way our mind categorises information – our "Categories of the Mind". On the other hand, Mitchell makes the warning that religious people should not make their beliefs "vacuous formulae" that is so vague they make no real impact on life, in the same way as those early astrologers made their claims and predictions so vague that they could alter them to accommodate any new conflicting evidence. *The candidate has used Mitchell well and connected his view to Popper's challenge of astrologers It would have been a good idea to include Mitchell's parable here.* Flew says that religious believers do the same, and that God died a "death of a thousand qualifications", because religious people simply change their beliefs to suit the challenges, and so is irrelevant and an issue for religious belief. *A well justified point rounding off the paragraph.*

In conclusion, it is clear that falsification can be used to some degree in an attempt to challenge religious belief, such as Flew's ideas of a thousand qualifications. However, Popper's foundational view that falsification should only serve to demarcate shows that religious belief can be supported by falsification by saying that it simply does not qualify for scientific scrutiny. Overall, this side of the argument seems more convincing and allows for science and religion to coexist as separate entities, thus meaning that the falsification principle does not present any real challenge to religious belief.

The candidate has summed up the case for and against and drawn a justified conclusion.

Overall 38/40, Grade A*

AO1: 14/16

The essay has been written concisely and presented in a very structured format. This is an excellent answer in that the candidate does not waste time with needless details but goes right to the heart of the debate and addresses scholars in a battle of arguments to discern the justified conclusion. However, the candidate should have used the falsification parables in this essay; while it is unnecessary to write pages on the explorers or the lunatic and the dons, it is expected that the candidate explains how they are used to justify the scholars' conclusions. Additionally, the candidate seemed more concerned with God-talk and less with religious belief which, while mentioned, was not effectively analysed. Something like the following would have been beneficial: "In an attempt to demonstrate that God-talk is meaningless, Flew sought to undermine the whole basis of religious belief; if one cannot talk about God, then one has no basis within which to believe in God." And to defend religious belief: "Hare's bliks show us that it is the believer that stipulates what evidence can be counted towards or against his/her belief; as with the lunatic and the dons, one's blik affects not only how one speaks but how one lives their life and a believer's blik, e.g. 'God loves me' certainly affects a believer's life and no scientific proof will have a chance at undermining that believe without the believer's permission."

Despite this, however, the candidate has shown excellent knowledge of the scholars and their positions on the debate; in using the scholars' views in defence and response to each other, the candidate has shown excellent understanding of the concepts and how they relate to each other, e.g. how bliks and Language Games compare etc. The candidate has selected specific ideas for this essay, but should have really included the parables to better demonstrate the scholars' views and justify their conclusions. Finally, terminology and language was used to a sophisticated manner.

AO2: 24/24

The candidate has shown excellent analysis and evaluation throughout this essay making connections and comparisons between all the theories and scholars. The candidate fully engaged with the question from the outset presenting the positions of the debate well in the introduction and then linking back to the question at the end of each paragraph. Material was used that was beyond what is expected, e.g. the mention of Alston and Gould. Each stage of the debate was well defended and challenged showing critical analysis at every stage. Finally, the candidate showed each scholar's position clearly and evaluated throughout.

'God talk is meaningless'. Discuss. (40/40 Grade A*)

This essay is not done under timed conditions but we have included it as it gives an excellent example of how to structure a complex argument. You could always try and write shorter version under timed conditions, extracting the key points.

Scholars have held this topic in strong debate in recent eras, through the formation of the Vienna Circle, many philosophers gathered together to discuss logical positivism and its application in the world today. This has been an ideal communicated within many works of literature such as Orwell discusses in "1984" where the talks of how the ideas in the mind are inextricably linked to language. Logical positivism covers a number of philosophical positions such as from A.J Ayer's Verificationism and Falsification to Wittgenstein's Language Games. Moritz Schlick was an imperative figure in the establishment of the Vienna Circle, he maintained that if you cannot demonstrate with sense observation how a statement is true, and then it is factually meaningless. God talk therefore is meaningless as by these criteria there is no way to instantiate the subject. Nevertheless this position has been criticised on several grounds by many including Hick who states that religious language can in fact meet the criteria for verificationism.

This is an excellent introduction which considers the context and background of the question and considers the Vienna Circle, which was where the Logical Positivist movement emerged. The candidate has mentioned Falsification in a question specifically focused on the meaningfulness and meaninglessness of language which is typically directed towards Verificationism. However, Falsificationism can be used if done so correctly. A thesis statement identifying the line of reasoning to be followed would be beneficial here.

A.J. Ayer was a logical positivist, much like his non cognitive approach to Emotivism on Meta ethics, he believed that putative propositions can only be literally meaningful once they have been analytically and empirically verified, this is the basis of verificationism. *Slight correction: propositions can only be meaningful if they can be verified or falsified (this is not reference to Falsificationism just yet, only that if something cannot be proven to be true, it is false).* Much like Hume's Fork there are two strict criterions attached to strong verificationism: which states that something can only be conclusively verified through experience and observation. *Or through reason; strange that this was missed out. A good link back to Hume's Fork.* Firstly this philosophical movement claims that language is only meaningful if it can be verified by sense observation (tapping into Anthony O'Hear's idea of checks and how one must be able to touch, see etc.) *Lovely nuance.* Secondly, statements can be verified if it is a tautological or analytical statement – whereby it is self-definable. For instance a bachelor is an unmarried man, is self-evident by the definition of a bachelor. To say that a car is red can be verified – as you can use your senses to deduce at a conclusion that the car is in fact red. However to say something more abstract such as the car is beautiful, is an opinion therefore it is unverifiable and so it is meaningless. Ayer claimed that when discussing God Talk – it may be "emotionally significant to him; but it is not literally significant".

This is a very good paragraph in that it overviews the whole position of logical positivism.

God talk therefore is meaningless as by these criteria there is no way to instantiate the subject as we are in fact talking about an ethereal being transcendent to human observation. It is therefore more probable that we should talk of God rather than stating what God is – state what he is not, using Via Negativa; for instance if we know that he is transcendent then it is much easier to ascertain that he is therefore not mortal and has no body than to say that he is good or he is powerful, this can be much easier gotten through the use of Via Negativa. This principle is not similar to that of verificationism; rather it maintains that God talk isn't meaningless, rather it states that we fall short in trying to define the nature of God as the language that we use to define God, is constricted to our own temporal barriers that cannot be accurately applied to eternal beings. While we can use parables to describe what we believe him to be like ultimately, he is ineffable and his nature cannot be truly defined. It is noteworthy that people have utilised this in many occasions when trying to express the ineffable such as accounts from St. Teresa of Avila where she communicates her religious experiences.

This is an interesting use of Via Negativa here. Typically one would not cross over to theological language in a question focused on Verification. However, given that Via Negativa in its own way supports the Verificationist notion that you cannot talk meaningfully of God in positive language, there is a cleaver and insightful link across. This could be defined more clearly though.

Strong verificationism however has been criticised, due to its lack of practical applications and the fact that it excludes universal statements such as water boils at 100 degrees, since we cannot boil all the water in the universe. This premise doesn't take into account things which we take for granted that cannot be verified, especially by one's self, however it doesn't in fact mean that these things are meaningless. Taking as an example a Black Raven, we generally accept that Ravens are black, yet by definition, this has to be so at all times, however this cannot be verified so it becomes meaningless. Swinburne then concluded that the same applies surely, when one talks about historical occurrences such as war, which too can be considered to be literally meaningless as there is no way to verify that they actually took place. It was at this point which Ayer responded with his principle of weak verification, which claims that the probability of all things being equal then so must that thing be, this takes the form of a more inductive argument, claiming that we don't need to kill everyone to check that people are mortal, simply we know this from other conclusive evidence that has led us to this assumption. This was however considered to be too liberal, allowing the verification of any statement. Whereas strong verificationism is like practical verifiability: where you can verify statements through sense experience yourself. Weak verificationism is more like verifiability in principle – whereby it claims that if we had the resources, then we could verify things. If we could for instance devise a time machine to take us back to the past, then we could in principle literally prove events such as the Battle of Hastings in 1066. Thus Hick challenges this maintaining that therefore religion is not meaningless because its truth is verifiable in principle, hence it meets the demands or the conditions of verificationism and God talk is thus not meaningless. If God were to exist then the verification of his existence is verifiable in principle, we simply just don't have the evidence. It is noteworthy that agnostics have pondered as to whether or not religious experiences can be considered evidence for God talk. However if God didn't in fact exist, then his existence is not falsifiable and you cannot prove that he doesn't exist. When discussing religious claims it becomes debatable as to whether there is enough proof of God's existence through weak verification. Ayer maintained that no statement which refers to a reality transcending the limits of all possible sense experience can possibly have any literal significance. Hence all god talk is meaningless.

This is a very well-structured paragraph, if rather long. It can be difficult to explore all the variations of Verificationism: strong and weak, principle and practice, direct and indirect. The candidate has made the exchange between Ayer and his critics the basis for this exploration which is clever and better than just listing the variations.

Things can be both directly and indirectly verifiable – if the first, it maintains that something is verified if it can be observed or such that it is in conjunction with one or more observational statements, (as you can't verify everything yourself.) indirect verificationism on the other hand means a statement that is not directly verifiable or analytic. This means that even though the statement cannot be verified alone, other independent verifiable statements act as evidence. Such as we cannot see Cancer in the body ourselves, however scans such as MRI can act as evidence to indirectly verify the claim that a patient has cancer. This is more commonly known as a deductive argument. Nevertheless claiming that statements are only meaningful if verifiable by sense observation is, itself an unverifiable claim that you cannot demonstrate in principle by sense observation. This ironically is the general criticism of this theory; however Swinburne also claims that matters that are logically unverifiable are still matters of meaning and importance, such as ethical decision making and Schrödinger's cat.

This paragraph is haphazardly begun, which is a shame as it is Ayer's final attempt at making sense of Verificationism. A good use of Swinburne here, though a reference to his toys in the cupboard would be better than Schrödinger's cat. Granted, the latter is in fact an excellent example in itself. Indirect Verification is about having evidence for something that you can't prove, so talking quantum physics would be an excellent rebuttal.

Another philosophy which is commonly referred to when dealing with matters such as this is falsification; this was instigated by Karl Popper. This maintains that if something is not scientific, it cannot be falsified. The truth or falseness of a statement can be tested by empirical observation of the universe, if a statement can't be falsified, then it is meaningless. This essentially means that you have to make an attempt at proving something to be wrong – to prove that it is without a doubt right. An interesting example of where falsification is prominently explained is through astrology, astrologers were impressed yet also mislead by what they believed to be confirming evidence. They also tended to be unimpressed by unfavourable evidence. They made their interpretations so vague that they were able to explain away anything that might have been a refutation of their theory this avoided falsification as they destroyed the testability of their theory, hence it became irrefutable. Popper talked about how falsification is about demarcating or (Setting apart) scientific claims from other claims. The criterion of falsifiability is a solution to the problem of demarcation, as it states that statements in order to be ranked as scientific must be capable of conflicting with possible or conceivable observations. Therefore if a statement cannot be falsified then it is not scientific and is meaningless. The principle difference between verificationism and falsification is the use of empirical evidence. While if something is proved empirically, then it is verified. If you disprove something empirically it is falsified and vice versa. Anthony Flew contributed to this idea of falsification. He stated that believers will allow nothing to falsify their claims and beliefs of God; therefore God talk is meaningless as it is unfalsifiable. He maintained that "God dies a death of a thousand qualifications", as whenever a believer's definition of God is challenged, the definition is changed to suit the challenge. "The believer's earlier statement had been so eroded by qualification that it was no longer an assertion at all". John Wisdom also added on to this stating that to talk about the nature of God is totally outside of the traditional methods of scientific enquiry hence does this make it meaningless? In reference to Boethius, he stated that knowledge of God's nature is beyond human comprehension.

The candidate has expertly introduced the position of Falsification. In its first form it did not speak out against god-talk as Popper was concerned with pseudo-science. It is Flew's interpretation that brings it into this essay as he claims that unfalsifiable statements area meaningless. Lovely use of Wisdom.

Here the parable of the invisible Gardener is used, where two people talk of how they returned to a neglected garden to find that some plants are still growing healthily the claimant claims that there could be a gardener that came to water the plants, yet the other doubts this. So they search for the gardener. When there is none, the claimant then adds that he is invisible and when this is disproven through the use of bloodhounds, again he adds that he cannot also be smelt. This shows how God is constantly being redefined in definition, and what we are left with is that the statement is so removed from its original assertion that it is no longer one.

It would be a nice addition to mention that this was Wisdom's parable which Flew used in his attack on god-talk.

Hare also talked about a Blik, this is a claim about the world that is not falsifiable nor can it be tested. Bliks are ways of seeing the world and the difference between different people's Bliks cannot be solved by observation of what the world is like. Conflicting Bliks cannot be settled through rationale, reason or experience. He utilised the parable of the paranoid lunatic who is convinced that all the dons (Professors) are trying to kill him, even when introduced to the nicest don – he maintains that this is his cunning plan. This parable is communicating to us that only the claimant has the authority to determine what evidence is acceptable, therefore making it unfalsifiable. Flew does however make the mistake of treating religious statements as though they are scientific explanations. He said that Christians make assertions about the universe, assertions are claims such as "God made the universe". Christians don't however claim that this is a Blik – yet a falsifiable claim.

A clumsy opening to this paragraph. There should be more of an organic link between paragraphs. This paragraph is correct in that Christians are making statements about reality, not 'just' bliks. However, it should be noted that bliks are statements that can only be altered and changed by the claimant. That is vital to understanding their use. Only the claimant has the authority to alter and refute the blik and only they know what evidence, if any, would be enough to challenge it.

If we were to be presented with the right checks, we would even doubt our most core beliefs. For instance to see adoption papers, we would believe that our mother is not our mother. Yet one wouldn't simply dismiss this, thus would check to see if the adoption papers are veridical, if they were, then we would know they aren't our parents. Yet this is not so for Christians in terms of God? So it is un-falsifiable hence making God Talk meaningless. Mitchell said that theists do not accept evidence that goes against their beliefs. Believers have to take care that religious beliefs are not just based on blind faith alone therefore making them irrational and unfalsifiable. To illustrate this point, he uses the parable of the stranger and the Partisan. They meet one night and the partisan is greatly impressed with him. The stranger helps members of the resistance yet he also aids the police, still the partisan maintains that he is on our side (regardless of them not meeting in these conditions again). The sceptic's however ask what would have to be done for you to see that he is not on our side? The partisan refuses to answer. The difference between the invisible gardener and the stranger and the partisan parable is that in the first, the claimant is constantly re-qualifying the claim making it unfalsifiable. Yet secondly, the claimant maintains the claim despite contrary evidence hence holds a blind faith position – which isn't rational, hence unfalsifiable.

This is all correct, however, there is no link back to the question and so its use in the essay is lost slightly. What does this parable say in terms of meaningfulness of god-talk?

Finally in contrast to this, Wittgenstein proposed his philosophy of Language Games, in which he talks about how to image a language is to imagine a form of life. He believed that language made sense only within its specific contexts and therefore couldn't be subject to verification. Similarly to a game of Chess, it has rules which govern the pieces but those same rules would not make any sense in football if applied there. The same goes for language; words are governed by rules such as grammar and syntax and only make sense in a certain context – when people are in dialogue. The use of language according to Wittgenstein was not a private but a public use. Therefore in reference to God talk, when theists claim statements such as "God is real or alive" it is meaningful as it is being used in a context which makes sense. Theories such as verification aren't applicable to religious language, since they concern a language game in which sense observation is the context; yet religious language is not concerned with sense observation so the language is different. This adds support to the claim that religious language (God talk) is meaningful.

A good use of Wittgenstein. He is the crux around which this topic balances. It would be pertinent and clever to link Language Games to bliks: bliks are personalised positions, language games are shared ones.

Nevertheless there have been challenges to this view, and it mainly states that this type of philosophy allows anyone to speak about God without feeling obliged to verify their claims empirically. In doing so it removes the link between religious language and empirical evidence is such a way that religious claims may not be taken seriously by empiricists. It is noteworthy that when a theist claims that God is real, they do not mean it in an emotional sense – they mean it empirically. That being said, Wittgenstein's insistence that language is a communal activity, not a private one certainly emphasises the communal essence present in religious language for instance Baptism, Salat etc – are all religious words which find their true meanings in community not private isolation. In his later works Wittgenstein writes about how it is difficult to realise the groundlessness of our believing on certainty – talking about how much mere acceptance on the basis of no evidence forms our lives. Present day philosophers are more likely to challenge religion as opposed to science, as they are deluded into thinking that science can justify its own framework.

This should be brought right back to Wisdom and how God is beyond normal everyday language. Additionally, an excellent insight would be to link this to Popper's Falsification and how we demarcate between science-talk, maths-talk, music-talk and god-talk etc.

Evidently therefore, it is clear to see that when one makes the assertion that

God talk is meaningless, they are doing so due to the unverifiability of such claims. Surely as we cannot instantiate the subject as we are in fact talking about an ethereal being transcendent to human observation, then it is meaningless to talk about? However this premise doesn't take into account things which we take for granted that cannot be verified, especially by one's self, for instance we cannot verify that historically some things occurred. This opened the door to weak verificationism which is more of an inductive argument, maintaining that all things being equal it could be veridical through other sources of evidence. Therefore in principle – religious claims could be verified hence they have meaning. Many scholars have attached their ideas to the principle of falsification, which attempts to disprove religious claims through its unscientific testable nature. They claim that religious claims always fall into similar mistakes, either God dies a death by a thousand qualifications as the original assertion is always being redefined that it becomes eroded by its qualifications, or some people take talk of God to heart through blind faith, never truly understanding it – which is what Mitchell warns us against or people simply refuse to accept other's knowledge maintaining that it is within their Blik's not to accept this information. Nevertheless Wittgenstein challenges this maintaining that religious language is not concerned with sense observation so the language is different. The same way that different games abide by different rules, so too does this hence theories such as verificationism isn't applicable to religious language. This adds support to the claim that God talk is meaningful.

Overall: A [40/40]*

An excellent summary of the two positions and the varied perspectives within them drawing upon all that has been said to arrive at a satisfying conclusion.

AO1: 16/16

The candidate has shown excellent comprehension and focus on the question. The knowledge and understanding of that knowledge is shown throughout with use of varied scholars and scholarly opinions, both on the syllabus and off. The material selected only aids in answering the question and showing the candidate's ability to argue the different perspectives. The essay is packed with knowledge.

AO2: 24/24

The candidate has shown an excellent ability to argue the positions of the debate and answer the question at every step. Each position is analysed thoroughly and expertly with precision and focus. Each view is developed and nothing is left asserted without justification. There are clever insights between scholarly views, even if some were missed. The line of reasoning, though not identified in the introduction, grows out of the way the essay is written so that the read arrives at the conclusion knowing that this is the destination.

Ethics H573/2

In the Ethics syllabus we are considering four general issues, and in the exam you will need to weave these issues together and evaluate the theories behind them.

1. How are norms (values of good and bad) derived? Values have to come from somewhere - either by an a posteriori route (the experience of pleasure and pain as in utilitarianism), an a priori route (Kantian ethics), through intuitions (intuitionism), or from God (some kind of Divine Command Theory, or an inbuilt, designed moral sense as in natural law).

2. How are these norms applied to such issues as euthanasia, business ethics, or sexual ethics? Is it practical to use a maximising principle (the Greatest Happiness Principle) or Kant's imaginative step of universalising our behaviour?

3. Are the moral theories we study realistic? Do they fit our idea of what motivates us? For example, is situation ethics and its emphasis on agape love just too idealistic and difficult to be useful? Is there always an element of *self-interest*?

4. What is the foundation of ethics? Does it lie with God, or in the natural world, or in experience? Moreover, what do the words 'good' and 'bad' actually mean? This is the concern of meta-ethics (literally beyond *normative* ethics).

Notice that there are synoptic links we can make between the three papers. For example, the argument from design (the teleological argument) links with Dawkins' argument that nature has no purpose (Christian Thought) and the natural law view in ethics (that there is a human nature designed by God to orientate us towards the good - the synderesis principle).

Kantian ethics argues for an a priori method - so does the ontological argument for God's existence. Hick was inspired by Kant's noumenal realm - the realm we cannot access by the senses where ultimate reality lies - to form his theory of universal pluralism (Christian Thought). Hick's idea is that God represents the ultimate 'noumena' or unaccessible divine reality, and we get glimpses from all world religions both of this truth, and in our religious experience of the divine.

To what extent, if any, is Utilitarianism a good theory for approaching moral decisions in life? (30/40 Grade B)

Arguably, the use of utilitarianism for the making of moral decisions is more detrimental to a society than it is beneficial. Indeed the very basis on which utilitarianism is founded, 'happiness' or 'pleasure', proves to be the first stumbling block. The 'paradox of hedonism' suggests that pleasure itself cannot be directly obtained. Instead, we must aim for more substantial conclusions, such as wealth or power - pleasure is merely a symptom that follows. This idea is most acutely explained by politician William Bennett: 'Happiness is like a cat, If you try to coax it or call it, it will avoid you; it will never come. But if you pay no attention to it and go about your business, you'll find it rubbing against your legs and jumping into your lap.'

Good. Excellent summary of the utilitarian problem that once you pursue happiness or pleasure as an end in itself it tends to elude you.

Therefore, to base one's entire ethical approach to life on happiness, something which is so fleeting and indistinct, suddenly seems irrational. *You need to mention a philosopher here such as Mill and ground the argument in what he says.* If we cannot amass pleasure within ourselves, how can we be so vain as to assume we can recognise its form in others, particularly those we don't know (e.g. in the case of a politician forming their policies on utilitarian principles.) That is not to say that the 'pursuit of happiness' in a wider sense will always be futile, but that one should make decisions independently, on grounds other than those utilitarian, and allow happiness to follow.

Is it not true to say we can assess polices looking backwards with hindsight because all the consequences are known, but not forwards when there are often unintended consequences? This paragraph is too general to be of much analytical quality – make sure you go straight into a philosophical theory.

On the other hand, rule utilitarianism appears to offer a resolution. If one chooses to implement a pre-determined set of rules (e.g. to avoid lying, to be pacifistic, to be modest,) which predominantly bring about the most 'pleasure'/ good for society, then focus can be diverted away from pursuing *you mean personal happiness here* happiness, and instead towards living a righteous life.

Yes, but again, you need to give this a theoretical grounding in Mill's weak rule utilitarianism – Mill's point is we are foolish to ignore the experience of people who have gone before us in terms of general rules or guidelines for creating the happy society. But when moral dilemmas occur we revert to being act utilitarians.

Jeremy Bentham (the father of modern utilitarianism) was somewhat of a polymath - to suggest that he was solely a 'philosopher' would be a vast understatement. *This kind of comment is irrelevant to the question and a waste of time.* Undoubtedly, he was also a great social reformer, basing his beliefs on the underlying principle of egalitarianism (i.e. equality for all.) However, in many ways, utilitarianism innately contradicts 'egalité.'

This paragraph is a good example of the kind of paragraph a highly analytical essay never contains because you are merely describing the life and times of Mr Bentham and not adding anything to the argument.

Initially a thought experiment experiment devised by the American philosopher Robert Nozick, 'the utility monster,' undermines the very equality for which Bentham's philosophy once fought. Visualise a situation in which the hedonic calculus is being employed. In such a case, the intensity (quality) of the perceived happiness must be acknowledged. For illustration's sake, imagine rations are being distributed amongst a group of isolated individuals. However, one of these individuals appears to gain a disproportionately high intensity of pleasure on receiving food, despite all other individuals being of an equally critical state of health (e.g. starvation.) To apply the hedonic calculus would not only (unfairly) favour the minority, but also pose a great risk to the majority (assuming that the individual's pleasure is greater than the collective pleasure of the majority.)

Yes this is a good point but it wouldn't apply to Mill's theory because social utility would mean we need principles of justice, otherwise any of us would be permanently miserable at just the thought of a utility monster.

The most valid counterargument to which is proposed by the British philosopher Derek Parfit, arguing that the scale of happiness should be seen as asymptotic rather than linear. That is, the happiness of a utility monster cannot perpetually increase, but will eventually reach a point near enough to 'complete' happiness. Hence, such a being is not conceivable. This argument bears a strong resemblance to prioritarianism, which suggests that individuals on the lower end of the 'pleasure spectrum' will obtain a greater amount of happiness ('per unit of utility') than those closer to the reverse end.

Again a good point and actually illustrating what economists call the principle of diminishing marginal utility – we eventually have less and less satisfaction as an individual until at some point we experience no satisfaction at all.

Or, to some extent, the intensity of happiness could thereby be omitted from the hedonic calculus to account for the utility monster. However, there is also a troubling flaw with the seventh principle - 'extent,' or the amount of people that a particular moral choice may affect. Counterintuitively, the one society which utilitarianism does not appear to permit, is a microcosmic 'utopia.' When summating the pleasure of individuals, the greatest amount will be achieved, theoretically, by an extremely populous group with indifferent levels of happiness rather than a very small but extremely contented group. This is known as the 'repugnant conclusion.'

Interesting and unusual point. Which philosopher talks about this problem?

In counterargument one might say, 'the average pleasure should supersede the total amount of pleasure' for this particular instance. Yet this line of argument spawns issues of its own. A simple average can easily be skewed by extremities. Such that one individual in a state of euphoria would significantly raise the average happiness of his miserable counterparts. Under the aforementioned, atrocities such as slavery could feasibly be justified. What's the suffering of one thousand imprisoned subordinates if the overseer is delighted by the recent success of his cotton farm? Utilitarianism, in this context, seeks to diminish the more valuable pursuits (charity, liberal arts) over the happiness one gains through materialism (e.g. the wealth garnered from a cotton farm.)

Even if all the preceding shortcomings were to be deemed permissible, there is still a flaw which is perhaps the most pertinent of all. Humans, by their very nature, are unable to reliably predict consequence, and without consequence, the principle of utilitarianism is worthless. Given the nature of the 'ripple effect,' it would be naive to assume that every possible consequence of even the simplest of decisions could be accounted for. Or moreover, to predict the ways in which people would (potentially dangerously,) apply utilitarianism if it were to be adopted as a global ethic.

Yes, again a very good point.

Even attempting to apply such a primitive, nebulous philosophy to an infinite diversity of ethical decisions seems rather unrefined. Despite superficially appearing succinct and rational, the impracticalities of achieving 'the greatest amount of pleasure for the greatest number of people' cannot be overlooked. Indeed, utilitarianism is theoretically sound but there are far too many exceptional cases for it to be one's ruling principle.

Overall 30/40 75% Grade B

The essay has some very interesting points to make. However, it would not achieve an A* because the establishment of how the utilitarianism of Bentham and Mill actually works is rather thin. Particularly, there is little substance about how Mill's weak rule utilitarianism actually works, and how some argue that rule utilitarianism collapses into act utilitarianism. In terms of social benefits versus individual benefits the candidate needs to bring out how this operates in Mill's theory, and how he grounds the final chapter of his essay on justice as a fundamental prerequisite of the happy society. Mill also moves his whole argument much closer to Aristotle as he writes his essay – leading some to call him an inconsistent utilitarian because he can't quite decide whether to go for qualitative pleasures or another concept of long-term welfare that is closer to eudaimonia in Aristotelean thought. It is lighter on AO1 marks than AO2 but seems to miss some of the analytical steps necessary to be a really compelling argument.

AO1 Level 4 10/16

A good demonstration of knowledge and understanding. Addresses the question well. Good selection of relevant material, used appropriately on the whole. Mostly accurate knowledge which demonstrates good understanding of the material used, which should have reasonable amounts of depth or breadth. A good range of scholarly views.

It is 'good' because it contains a very strong critical thesis. But it is neither very good nor excellent because the precise detail of how Bentham's and Mills theories work is lacking – it is assumed rather than stated and established and analysed. For example, there is an interesting relationship in Mill between higher and lower pleasures and act and rue utilitarianism whereby we should, Mill argues, generally follow a rule which past experience suggest will maximise social happiness but when we face a moral dilemma we revert to being an act utilitarian. There is also an ambiguity in the question which is never considered – moral decisions for whom?

AO2 level 5 20/24

A very good demonstration of analysis and evaluation in response to the question. successful and clear analysis, evaluation and argument. Views very well stated, coherently developed and justified. There is a well–developed and sustained line of reasoning which is coherent, relevant and logically structured.

It would have been excellent if there had been a little more engagement with the academic philosophers who produce the arguments, rather than just the arguments themselves.

Utilitarianism provides a helpful method of moral decision making. Discuss. (26/40 Grade C)

I believe Mill has a morally acceptable approach to Utilitarianism because it focuses on a more qualitative approach. *This sentence is unclear. You're actually referring to his view of pleasure as the one intrinsic good, and that this idea needs to divide between higher and lower pleasures. You would have been better off referring to the justice issue, which you mention in the essay, and its connection to rules. I think maybe you misunderstand what qualitative means.* Whereas Bentham's focuses on a more quantitative approach which means he has a tyrannical perception on the minority. *The phrase 'tyrannical perception' is also unclear – you mean simply that his theory implies that the interests minority groups could be sacrificed to the greater happiness.* Thus, I see Utilitarianism as unhelpful because it suggests how easy it is to see happiness where it is far more complicated to predict and be certain that pleasure will arise.

You are trying hard to impose a structure on your answer which is a good idea. But you need to practise writing clearer sentences. For example, the sentence 'how easy it is to see happiness' doesn't really say what you mean, which is "happiness can be defined clearly, measured and then maximised as a social goal' or something like that.

I see Utilitarianism as wrong because it doesn't focus on the act or the quality of the outcome. Wrong is a moral word. Wrong in what sense? This means that Bentham may allow a bad act to happen to allow the greatest happiness to arise for a possible bad group of people. Try to write full sentences which should have a verb in them – the full stop here is actually a comma. Such as, a gang of five beating up an old war veteran. Bentham allows this because it creates the greatest happiness even though the act is obscene an emotive word – avoid this kind of writing just something like 'would be unacceptable to most of us because it creates suffering for innocent people'. Bentham supports the idea better to say "argues for" (of) act Utilitarianism. This means that a person's act is morally right if it produces the best possible results in that situation; implying the greatest happiness for the greatest number. Yes that's a clearer sentence. Bentham looks at the consequence and measures the greatness *greatest happiness* by using the Hedonic Calculus. This is a mathematical calculation used to work out how certain the happiness/pain could occur or the extent of the amount of people being affected. This is used to work out the usefulness of a situation but it's much harder to make the calculation than it seems. Should be a comma not a full stop. Such as, you can never predict the consequences and thus being certain of whether pain or pleasure arises is very hard to work out. Good point It is also hard to apply the Hedonic Calculus to modern world situations because it is very basic meaning what? and ambiguous to certain complicated scenarios. Redundant full stop should be a comma. Such as, applying Bentham's Hedonic Calculus to Embryology *be specific – embryology is a very general term* would be very difficult as it has only been around for a short while and to be certain if research on embryos is ethically correct and provides happiness completely depends on our societies society's personal opinions.

Good – you are trying to illustrate your argument with specific examples. Make them even more specific eg embryology needs grounding in a little detail – what aspect of embryology?

Mill argues that his view of Utilitarianism focuses on everyone through quality equally rather than quantity. Mill talks about higher and lower pleasures where higher is what distinguishes humans from other animals. This is because higher pleasures are of more intellectual quality like reading which makes humans unique whereas animals just have lower pleasures which means all they do is life requirements like sex and eating. *Yes.* Mill once said "it is better to be a human being dissatisfied than a pig satisfied" which suggests that even unhappy human beings have a greater importance than an irrelevant animal which has no near significance than the life of a human. *Good, you're explaining what Mill said, not just stating what he said.*Mill also talks about the rule of thumb. This means that if a decision greatly resembles a previous decision, you can use it as a 'rule of thumb' to avoid using Bentham's Hedonic Calculus in detail. *Yes. JO Urmson (1952) classifies Mill as a 'weak rule utilitarian', meaning, the rules can be broken when we face a moral dilemma.*This goes against Bentham's act Utilitarianism because we can use experience to cope with immeasurable situations which act Utilitarianism struggles to do. Mill also criticises Bentham's view by the example of sadistic thugs. *As far as I know Bentham never uses this example, or have I missed it?* Such as, if an innocent man was convicted of a horrible crime and was sent to prison. *Comma, not full stop* And then three guards tortured him for their pleasure. Bentham would allow this as the three guards' pleasure outweighs the innocent man's. *Yes, good.* Using Bentham's Hedonic Calculus would result in the guards *continuing* what they are doing because it provides the greatest happiness for the greatest number. In contrast to this, Mill has cleverly thought of the harm principle. The harm principle was a principle which allowed people to do an act that must not harm others. *The harm principle says – the only time it's okay to restrict another's liberty is to prevent harm to others. This isn't quite what you've said here.* This particularly focuses on the minority as they usually have the worst side of things.

As an evaluation, I believe Mill has the better side of the argument because he attempts to look after the minority *yes* and also tries to put forward a qualitative approach so everyone can have a balanced but fair outcome doesn't follow from the qualitative approach. Bentham allows any act which I believe is feeble leads to immoral outcomes *(feeble again is an emotive word best avoided)* because this can have an outcome of bad people receiving the greatest happiness. Mill's sadistic thug example of this shows just how tyrannical Bentham's theory is and thus should not be applied to any moral situation if bad people can receive the greatest happiness. As mentioned in my thesis, Bentham has a quantitative approach which doesn't always produce the greatest outcome *do you mean morally or in terms of happiness? If the outcome isn't greatest one morally, then we need to link that idea to some moral principle it breaks. The obvious one is justice. as bad people can have the better ending. This is not fair as any bad act could happen to good innocent people.*

Another reason why I don't believe Utilitarianism is helpful for moral-decision making is because it is very hard to predict the consequences of an act and it's very subjective. *'It' here means the judgment about future pleasure or happiness presumably?* This means Utilitarianism can't be measured because it's too vague to gain an answer if a certain situation is very perplexing. *Yes - what about an example?* However, Bentham uses the Hedonic Calculus consisting of the seven criteria to measure and attempt to predict the amount of pain or pleasure produced. Bentham mentioned "Nature has placed mankind under two sovereign masters, pleasure and pain". Here Bentham is talking about how pleasure and pain are two prominent aspects in our lives, rather than some authoritative controlling mechanism. Through our own experience and initiative, we try to avoid pain at all opportunities and try to strive towards pleasure. *Yes* This is the idea of hedonism which Bentham wants everyone to be motivated for. Thus, Bentham uses the Principle of Utility to motivate all people .

I don't think Bentham is trying to motivate anyone but to provide a psychological/ empirical basis for moral choices — so it is a theory of psychological motivation maybe in trying to achieve the greatest happiness of the greatest number Bentham neglects the sacrificial aspect - why should I care about you?

And this is what makes us strive to having better moral behaviour because behaving well and obediently usually leads to an outcome of pleasure and rewards. This can be a good aspect towards moral-decisions because if we are inclined towards pleasure, we will do what we can in our power to help others and promote our behaviour to the best outcome possible. This implies that humans naturally are inclined towards pleasure and not pain. This suggests that using the Hedonic Calculus can help us look for the best things in life and if it doesn't go to plan, we can reflect on our past actions via the Hedonic Calculus and make the correct choices in the future. This can be seen as a method of trial and error where people can learn from their previous mistakes and use their experience to help with similar situations in the future.

Good attempt to build up an analysis - the trial and error idea may be worth developing.

However, I can argue that you can never be sure if an act will make something happen. Such as, if you gave a homeless man twenty pounds to spend on food which you expect him to spend on, you would feel certain that the homeless man would feel appreciated and you would be sure that the homeless man would be happy immanently. However, we are not mind-readers and the homeless man could actually spend the money on drugs or cigarettes to help him cope with rejection or loneliness. *Good example* In a situation where many outcomes could arise, you can never predict what is going to happen. In addition, it takes very a long time to actually work out all of the little aspects of which the Hedonic Calculus consists of. It would just be better to do a good act and know for sure pleasure will happen. To waste your time just trying to work out if the act is good in this situation is pointless. One could argue it would just be better to give the homeless man food so you know they have the right resources to keep them going. *Yes* And if you are trying to apply this theory to embryology or any modern method, it would be time consuming and hard to work out as this theory is based from a very long time ago where society was very simple compared to today.

Good paragraph - but be careful of saying something is 'pointless' without explaining why exactly. If you leave the idea just hanging there it reads like very opinionated writing rather than true analysis.

As an evaluation, I believe that the Hedonic Calculus should not be used because it is hard to predict consequences and to be sure what things could happen from an act. *You are tending to repeat yourself.* Bernard Williams *this isn't Williams' argument – he argues against Utilitarianism because of the 'integrity objection' - look this up!* said that Utilitarianism is good because it seems reasonable to try and seek the greatest happiness. And this is clearly good because getting the greatest happiness for the greatest number is fantastic as you are pleasing the most people. Williams also suggests that we can have good guesses and predictions to get a rough idea of what possible outcomes could happen. Such as, if we tortured a terrorist to get answers of where a bomb is which could kill a thousand people. We can have a good idea that by doing this to one man would result in more pleasure for more people as no bomb is going off and we are only causing pain to one person. However, do note this again leaves out a minority and a clear reason why I can't see it being justifiable. Although this example is an extreme case, there are many scenarios like Mill's sadist thug example *Mill doesn't mention this example* showing how a minority group is left in pain and horror. Mill puts forward rule Utilitarianism which allows everyone to follow a set of rules which ensures all people abide to. *You're jumbling up various points* This ensures that an action is right if it conforms to a rule that leads to the greatest happiness. To link back to my thesis, it's clear that Bentham believes in the Hedonic Calculus but I can't see it as usable because it is hard to predict difficult situations and it takes up far too much time.

This paragraph could have been rewritten to make a lot more sense and also disentangle various points. This candidate needs to practise writing analytically and avoiding words like 'fantastic'.

A clear point for the usefulness of Utilitarianism is because it's secular. This means it is not connected with religious or spiritual matters. *Why does that make it "useful"?* This portrays the fact that Utilitarianism is a basic *meaning what exactly?* theory which is naturally created through human methodology. It doesn't rely on ancient scripts like the Bible or certain rules like the 10 commandments which everyone must follow. *Fine* Bentham tried to make it unique to everyone as everyone's pleasure are equal. This appeals to large masses of people because everyone can understand and relate to it. This is important because the greatest number of people always receive the greatest happiness. So, in a situation that requires everyone's morality to be put to the test. *Comma, not full stop* Such as, deciding whether a 16-year-old-girl should have an abortion. You could argue that having the child will ruin the young girls' education and she would be in no state of understanding parenthood. *Good, as you're using an example* You don't have to pay attention to religion like the belief that life beginning at the moment of conception too as Utilitarianism is secular. But the parents may want the child and see it as unfair to kill an infant. Here, Utilitarianism can be applied as there are rules to follow and thus you have a clear path to finding the right answers. It is also relative *why? If you introduce this as an idea you must explain it* which means it can be used in any situation. This makes Utilitarianism flexible because it can be useful to any situation and allows you to use the Hedonic Calculus to measure what pain and pleasure you may gain out of it.

However, Kant argues against this theory by saying that relativism is not in favour of absolute rules. *This sentence is muddled – you mean the opposite* This means that a rule is true in all situations which is not necessarily the best of things. This can be carless because it can lead to huge confrontation if both sides believe in opposite things. Kant also rejects emotions. This means that you can't judge someone based on their personal feelings. *No full stop but a comma* Such as, if you had a son who was a drug addict and the parents were emotionally attached to him. They are likely to buy him drugs to keep the son happy and working well because without his drugs he struggles to cope with stress and school. This is feeble because why would you ever promote drugs to your children? *Good* Kant is wise and thus uses the idea of reason to consolidate an answer. Kant would suggest the parents should say "We should look after our son's health by not buying him drugs and taking him to a doctor". This would seem the correct approach as you are using your initiative to get you through this tricky situation. Using emotions can also be seen as weak because you are using your own personal feelings to feel sorry for others. Such as, people succumbing to tears can be seen as a weakness because you are yielding to peoples' sadness whereas you should move on and follow what is right by using reason. If you are attempting to make a moral-decision, sympathising for emotion is illogical because this can make you feel sorry for others changing your views. *Good*

As an evaluation, I support Kant's argument because it is a logical rational approach because you are not yielding to peoples' personal feelings. *Not very well expressed - you mean Kant considers feelings of no moral worth because they are fickle.* You are using reason via experience to get through in life which is best. To a situation that requires a moral-decision to be made, reason is the most logical approach because it can be applied to any situation and is a useful method of working out what to do in certain situations. Although Utilitarianism is secular which means it doesn't rely on any other explanation or religious rule, it still doesn't include the minority. It provides no protection to the most vulnerable which Mill ensures does happen by the harm principle. *Explain the harm principle* It is evident that Mill has a more collective approach so everyone is considered. Bentham doesn't allow this as he has a main focus of ensuring that a majority gains the most happiness. This is why Mill supports the idea of rule Utilitarianism where you have a basic set of rulings to follow. This is so you know everyone has a legal obligation to follow from the start. Bentham is focused on pro-equality which is a positive but not all people always receive this. Linking to my thesis, it is never easy to predict the consequences of a situation making the Hedonic Calculus worthless in complicated situations. Bentham's approach is lacking in support for everyone which leaves out a minority and makes them vulnerable like children. This makes his theory very weak as there is no protection for children or the mentally sick. Mill uses the harm principle to back up the vulnerable and also ensures rules are set up beforehand so it's a fair approach to *what's the connection between rules and fairness?* any given situation.

Total 26/40 65% Grade C

This essay is a bit of a mixed bag. There are some very good elements – the attempt to impose a coherent thesis and the use of examples. But strategically you adopt the wrong approach to essay-writing because you try to say everything and so quite often the essay becomes a bit of a list where you are ticking off one point after another. You can't say everything and if you do, you end up being unclear about some points. This essay therefore often lacks clarity. An example would be the treatment of qualitative pleasure in Mill. You seem to misunderstand this, and as it's a central point (which you keep repeating) it weakens your argument.

A second good point is the interweaving of analysis and evaluation as AO2 skills – sometimes very good, on occasions less successful, but absolutely the right tactic.

A third good point is the attempt to construct a clear thesis.

So....the essay is too long, a bit too formulaic, unclear in places, and muddled/ unclear on qualitative pleasure. Don't try to say everything! It's important to practice writing shorter and tighter essays.

Grade B/C If you are a teacher reading this, make a judgement about whether to grade a bit higher to B to encourage someone who is trying very hard, but missing the mark sometimes. Marked objectively, I think it's a C grade that might just scrape a B if the grade bands were a little lower than usual.

AO1 Level 4 (10 marks) A good demonstration of knowledge and understanding. Addresses the question well. Good selection of relevant material, used appropriately on the whole. Mostly accurate knowledge which demonstrates good understanding of the material used, which should have reasonable amounts of depth or breadth. A good range of scholarly views

AO2 Level 4 (16 marks) A good demonstration of analysis and evaluation in response to the question. Generally successful analysis, evaluation and argument. Views well stated, with some development and justification. Answers the question set well. There is a well-developed line of reasoning which is clear, relevant and logically structured.

'Kantian ethics is helpful for moral decision-making in every kind of context.' Discuss (22/40 Grade D)

On one hand, I do not think that Kantian ethics is helpful with every decision. This is because all situations are different and are not the same so it cannot be universal. Kant's theology *why theology – don't you just mean Kant's ethics?* was based on very 'black and white terms' *this sort of phrase should be avoided as it's not very clear what it means, you really mean 'black and white applications of the categorical imperative'.* Which we normally term 'absolute' because they don't *change with circumstances* he focussed on the moral act of a situation and ignored the consequences that could be a result of that act. His theology also was based on the idea of Maxims. Maxims are moral rules that are determined by reason. He believed that everyone has reason and so if we all had reason then this makes us all the same, meaning that we all should be making the same moral decisions *No. Having reason doesn't mean we all agree when we make moral decisions..* An example of a maxim that Kant introduced was that 'lying is wrong and we should focus on always telling the absolute truth.' However, a flaw to this theory is when it is put into context, it contradicts itself. For example, the situation with the man and the axe. A murder with an axe in his hand has turned up to your house and he is asking you 'where is your mother I am going to kill her?' In this situation, Kant would say that you should tell the truth of where the mother is, regardless of the consequences (mother would die). I think that the maxims that Kant put in place aren't specific enough to each situation because every situation is unique. Universal rules aren't helpful in the real world because every situation is different. *(Repetition is unnecessary and actually detracts from analytical writing)* There are never two situations that are the same. Therefore, the theory should be relativist and not absolutist. Overall, I think that Kantian ethics should not be applied when making every moral decision because it doesn't take into consideration the situation that the individual is in, therefore it isn't universal because the rules are too set in stone.

Phew! We have a number of excellent points here, but as a writing tactic, it's not a good idea to have an opening paragraph that tries to say so much. Why not just say 'there are three reasons why Kant's ethics is unworkable. Then spell out the three reasons in a subsequent paragraph structure. You are overloading the opening paragraph with analytical and evaluative points which makes the essay in danger of losing the power of the argument. What does this question mean by 'every context'? The place of the opening paragraph is to address this kind of ambiguity in the question.

On the counter side, Kantian ethics is reliable in some circumstances *hopefully you will make these 'circumstances' clear!*. It relies on a system of rules which is very clear cut, meaning that everyone is aware of the obligations. *Yes, but you need to show me how Kant produces the rule in the first place! By a priori reason.* If you allowed everyone to break the rules, then the consequences of the legal system would be a mess. *Moral law is not the same thing as the legal system. The legal system takes a case by case approach anyway – you can kill someone in self-defence for example.* No one would know what they ought to do. For example, in order for everyone to do their duty, it must be able to be universalised. In other words, the individual has to think to themselves "can I apply this to all situations/ circumstances?" To put this in context, making a lying promise about loaning some money. i.e. if you promise to take a loan of money out with the intention that you will not be able to pay the company back in the time that has been given, the promise contradicts the act of keeping a promise. *Yes, technically he calls this a perfect duty because it is logically contradictory to break the rule of promising as, if broken, it destroys the idea of promising itself* Kant would view this as it being morally wrong to make a lying promise and so would advise people not to take a loan out because one may not be able to guarantee that they can pay the company that leant the money back. This therefore supported Kant's idea that lying contradicts itself. *This is the obvious place for a paragraph break* However, on the other hand others may argue that Kant's theology is inflexible. It should be able to break an unhelpful rule if the individual circumstances mean that that is the right thing to do. For example, going back to talking about the example with making a lying promise. In some situations, a person may want to take out a loan and would be able to pay the money back and so they may not be able to because of universal moral laws that have been put in place which say that this is wrong. Therefore, I think that this is unrealistic because Kant asks us to follow maxims, but sometimes just because some people act in one way doesn't mean that others will. Just like the person who will take out a loan even though they know that they will not be able to pay the money back. Overall, I think that Kantian ethics are helpful for moral decision-making in some contexts because it is so clear that a child could understand what they should and should not do . This means that no one can act in a selfish way and so would promote a happier environment.

This paragraph has some good analytical and evaluative points mixed in. However, the paragraph is still too long. It suggests to me that you aren't planning your answer properly.

Another strength in Kant's theory that is helpful for moral decision-making is that his theory supports equality and justice *don't you mean equality and justice for all?*. In other words, Kant's theory provides a basis for Human rights. In 1948, UN Declaration of Human rights was agreed by 48 countries and is the world's most translated document, protecting humans around the globe. This means that the theory provides the foundations for modern conceptions of equality and justice and suggests that no one can be used for being a different race, culture or religion. It also suggests that everyone is of equal worth and that no one is of a higher value of another individual. *That point comes before* the equality and justice point because the two ideas stem from the second formula – the formula of ends which you need to explain more fully. This as a result would reduce the chances of social unsettlement *(strange word)* and minimise the amount of prejudice that is happening in the modern day. However, this is not always the case. For example, in today's world prejudice and discrimination is still happening in some countries even though there are moral laws in place which say that this is not acceptable. And so, even though there are laws in place, it doesn't necessarily mean that everyone is going to abide by the rules. This therefore means that an unrealistically high standard is set which some people are not adhering to which was always going to be the case otherwise there would be no need for moral laws to be put in place. To conclude this, I still think that Kantian ethics is helpful for some moral decision-making but not in every kind of context. My reason for this I because not everyone makes moral decisions and it cannot be universalised because the rules are not universal in all situations and so it is unrealistic.

Total 22/40 55% Grade D

Plenty of good ideas not every well developed or knitted together. This candidate needs to work on both structure and analysis/evaluation to improve to the standard of a B or A grade. Points need to be separated into a more logical structure of thought, rather than trying to say everything at once. The opening and closing paragraphs need to be worked on – indeed – the idea of a paragraph itself doesn't seem to be grasped. Underlying this there is some attempt to ground points in practical examples. There are also some confusions here which bring this essay down to a D grade answer (the lack of structure being another factor on top of this). For example the student here seems to think universal is the same as universalisable – which they definitely aren't – and that as a result we would all produce the same application of the categorical imperative. This is not Kant's point – his point is that each of us can and should make the moral law for ourselves and not rely on others. We are autonomous and use a priori reason to create our own categoricals. We will share some of these – such as lying is wrong, but others may be different (the imperfect duties for example).

A final point – the only example discussed in depth is the crazy axe murderer – but this needs to be in the bulk of the essay and an example of the problem Kantian ethics seems to produce when two 'goods' conflict (such as breaking a promise to run an errand after school because someone has just collapsed in the street) isn't addressed. Do Kantian categoricals always collapse into hypotheticals when a specific situation is addressed?

AO1 Level 3 (10 marks)

A satisfactory demonstration of knowledge and understanding with use of mostly relevant material. Some accurate knowledge demonstrating understanding through material used but may be lacking in breadth. Sources - academic approaches are used to demonstrate knowledge and understanding with only partial success. There aren't many academic views mentioned at all. Too much 'opinion' with not enough substantiation by specific reference to another philosopher or academic's viewpoint.

AO2 Level 3 (12 marks)

A just about satisfactory demonstration of analysis and/evaluation in response to the question. Some successful argument. Partially successful analysis and evaluation. Views asserted but often not fully justified. Mostly answers the set question. There is a line of reasoning presented which is mostly relevant and which has some structure. The paragraphing is poor.

'Natural law theory succeeds because it takes human nature seriously,' Discuss (36/40 Grade A*)

The proposition that 'natural law theory succeeds because it takes human nature seriously' is flawed from the outset, because it makes the naive assumption that human nature is distinct and identical for all individuals. *Good – a very clear example of a thesis statement.* To some extent, its basis is fairly sound, that we should use a combination of what is natural and what is reasonable to form ethical decisions. But a theory which relies so heavily on something as subjective as human nature/reason is too malleable to be successful (i.e. reliable, uniform or justifiable.)

'Subjective' here probably means 'relative to culture and the ways of thinking produced by culture'. This link needs to be made explicit. But it's a very clear and concise opening paragraph.

Indeed, this is similar to the argument of Saint Augustine, who suggests that natural law is too optimistic a view of human nature. For a theory somewhat aligned with Christianity (due to its development by Thomas Aquinas,) it seems to contradict biblical teachings. *Actually Aquinas' theory became the 'semi-official moral theology of the Catholic church' (Peter Singer) and is reproduced in many encyclicals such as Veritatis Splendor (1995).* More specifically, Genesis: our inclinations cannot be trusted as we are all misguided by original sin. But this argument *(you mean criticism?)* is also valid from a more secular standpoint, in that human nature can never truly be perfect (e.g. due to imperfections in upbringing, culture, genetics or perhaps the more Platonic 'doxa.') *This doxa point needs explanation.* Therefore, one might say 'Natural law succeeds in spite of taking human nature seriously.' However, there are more glaring flaws,

115

unrelated to the problem of human nature.

Good critical/evaluative writing.

G.E Moore proposes (in 'Principia Ethica') that natural law is *commits* a 'naturalistic fallacy.' That is to say goodness, in and of itself, is unnatural and hence cannot be defined (i.e. it is merely a human construct.) *Moore uses the word 'non-natural' which has a preciser meaning from 'unnatural'.* To strive towards the (natural) goodness perceived by our human nature is irrational, because goodness itself is created, not discovered. This bears a strong resemblance to Scottish philosopher Hume's 'is-ought' criticism. Which recommends that we cannot reason how a given thing 'ought' to be based on how it currently 'is'; contradicting Aquinas' view that ethics can formed based on introspection (i.e. by observing the 'workings of the machine.')

It's good to link Moore and Hume although many philosophers argue that Hume's is a 'suppressed premise' argument, that people move too readily from is to ought without explaining themselves. As most moral theories are naturalistic., we can only assume that they supply the missing premise eg explaining why pleasure is 'good' and 'desirable'.

On the other hand, 'ought' is already very much akin to 'is.' Namely, because we know how something is, we must also know how it ought to be - most things have an objective/end-goal which is essential to their definition. American author McInerny uses the example of a clock: if one knows the definition of a clock, one can say 'because it 'is' a clock, it 'ought' to tell the time.' In this way, by taking human nature seriously, we can make seemingly successful conclusions.

Good – exactly the point, here place in a natural law, teleological context. Not only do human beings seem to act according to purposes, but they can justify those purposes with a moral argument. Never simply state that the naturalistic fallacy proves anything without also criticising the fallacy itself. John Searle is one philosopher who does this - look him up.

Furthermore, *(notice how analytical writing is characterised by the use of words such as 'furthermore – implying you will be pushing the point into even more interesting, A* territory),* for a theory to be 'successful,' it must be able to be applied with relative ease for all individuals to whom the ethic applies. This, Kai Nielson argues, is not achieved by natural law. For, in order to take human nature seriously, it must be taken into account for all people. And although these inclinations are similar amongst people of one nation, they are able to vary vastly between cultures. The disparity between these moral standards is described by Nielson as 'cultural relativism.' Such that in one culture it may be natural and logical to cremate a father's remains (on applying natural law,) in another it may only be culturally acceptable to bury familial remains.

Again, an interesting argument. You might also have introduced the problem of what to do when two moral goods conflict – as they often do as human nature seems to be in conflict between our passions and our reason. A double synoptic link could be made here to Plato's charioteer where the charioteer is attempting to control the black horse of passion/cravings and the white horse of our emotions/ noble sentiments, or the idea in Freud of a conscience which is trying continually to resolve conflicts. Note how this student continually makes reference to additional philosophers and academics. This is evidence of A grade writing.

A counterargument more crude, but equally as effective, comes from Peter Vardy's 'The Puzzle of Ethics' and criticises the simplicity of natural law. For it fails to take into account the deluge of contributing factors essential to making ethical decisions (instinct, emotion, reason etc.) Thus, to adhere to a primary precept such as 'preserve life' can prove problematic. Imagine the case of a terrorist, who must be tortured (and consequently killed) to preserve the life of many innocents. Natural law would conclude that the perpetrator could not be killed for it is a deontological theory, based on the rightness/wrongness of particular inclinations as opposed to that of consequences. Therefore, by committing to a primary precept, more life may be destroyed than preserved.

Actually natural law is partially consequentialist because, when assessing a double effect, you have to consider the end result or consequence of an action. The omission of a discussion of double effect is beginning to appear quite significant in this answer – remember that it was Aquinas who first introduced the idea as being a way of bringing human reason to bear on the complexity of life. This human reason is itself God-given and part of the divine image in us.

However, to a certain extent, some ethically dubious scenarios can be circumvented by use of the 'double effect doctrine.' As this was first referenced in Aquinas' 'Summa Theologica,' it is often used in conjunction with natural law. However, it is contingent on four conditions:

From the new Catholic Encyclopedia: *(Lists don't help analysis and should be avoided at all costs)*

1) The act itself must be morally good or at least indifferent.

2) The agent may not positively will the bad effect but may permit it. If he could attain the good effect without the bad effect he should do so. The bad effect is sometimes said to be indirectly voluntary.

3) The good effect must flow from the action at least as immediately (in the order of causality, though not necessarily in the order of time) as the bad effect. In other words the good effect must be produced directly by the action, not by the bad effect. Otherwise the agent would be using a bad means to a good end, which is never allowed.

4) The good effect must be sufficiently desirable to compensate for the allowing of the bad effect

This aims to overcome the aforementioned issue with primary precepts such as 'preserve life' by allowing for unintentional negative side effects.

At last and in the nick of time, the student introduces double effect. But remember to say it makes natural law truer to reason and experience and hence our rational human natures.

A good example of its application would be the 'trolley problem' (first devised by Philippa Foot,) which would allow the five to be saved, by sacrifice of the one. As the intention is not to destroy life, an action can be taken which minimises the bad effects of a situation. If one were to strictly follow the primary precept 'preserve life,' they may instead conclude that it is wrong to switch the trolley onto a route containing the innocent worker (thereby causing the death of the five.)

Good example. A grade answers use strong examples which are fully integrated into the analysis.

Hence, to create an ethical theory which takes human nature seriously is flawed because it relies on the metaphysic that 'all humans have some overriding shared purpose' which, on introspection,   leads to the creation of primary and secondary precepts. Indeed, natural law's second fundamental component, the use of reason, is also flawed for the ambiguity and diversity of human reasoning. Arguably, it is a well-intentioned theory which promotes self-analysis and a flourishing life (eudaimonia,) but it is perhaps the difficulties in its application which makes it ultimately unsuccessful.

Mark: 36/40 A (90%)*

Excellent strong conclusion. Overall a very good and at times excellent answer hovering between A grade and A. The excellence is reflected in the clarity of the argument and the very strong sequential feel to the way the writer develops the* *ideas – one idea does very definitely lead on to another. If you're having trouble developing a philosophical style, try to copy this writer's use of key link words and phrases (see the appendix at the back of this book). Also excellent is the use of additional academics/philosophers – although why not learn one or two quotes? They don't have to be long ones, or 100% accurate. Also notice how the writer never loses sight of the question or the interpretation (thesis) imposed on the question. That is the key to good philosophical writing.*

However: if you re-read the argument you will see that occasionally it is overstated. A good example is the reference to natural law being 'non-consequential" as this is a misunderstanding both of natural law itself ,and the role of right judgment within natural law, and its relation to the secondary precepts which are never absolute in Aquinas' thought. So, because the writer misunderstands this point, on this occasion a quite serious overstatement occurs. The phrase we use for this is 'lack of nuance'. Understanding some of these subtler points helps us not to overstate the case – and an overstated case is not quite an excellent one. It is nonetheless a very good essay.

AO1 Level 6 (14 marks) An excellent attempt to address the question showing understanding and engagement with the material; excellent ability to select and deploy relevant information. Extensive range of scholarly views, academic approaches, and/or sources of wisdom and authority are used to demonstrate knowledge and understanding

AO2 Level 6 (22 marks) An excellent demonstration of analysis and evaluation in response to the question. Confident and insightful critical analysis and detailed evaluation of the issue. Views skilfully and clearly stated, coherently developed and justified. Excellent line of reasoning, well-developed and sustained, which is coherent, relevant and logical.

Critically asses the view that businesses have a moral duty to put their customers first. (20/40 Grade D)

In this essay i will evaluate the extent that businesses have a moral duty to put their customers first *using the moral theories of utilitarianism and ….this is a classic example of a question that needs narrowing down – your decision remains as to how you narrow the question* I believe that businesses do have a moral duty to put their customers first as it is the customers that give money to a business and if therefore should be respected and given the best treatment. Corporate social responsibility is a sense that businesses have wider responsibilities than simply to their shareholders including the communities they live and work in. in this essay I will also be taking CSR into account for some of the arguments.

Many questions are begged by the exam question itself. This question, for example, begs the question – what does it mean to put the customer first? If it means for example, the business loses money, then the business will cease to exist. In practice, therefore, there may be a trade off between profit and perfection of the relationship with the customer. Milton Friedman's views might have been mentioned even in the opening paragraph, as he argues that profit has to come first in a capitalist market economy – as a tactic I would always mention a counterpoint (and a name of someone else) in the opening paragraph to whet the examiner's appetite.

Utilitarianism would also agree that businesses have a moral duty to put their customers first. This is due to utilitarianism being based around the greatest happiness for the greatest number. By having that theory in mind leads us to believe that for a business to make the most people happy then the customers would be included in that. *Yes, but so would all stakeholders – worth bringing in stakeholder theory here* Businesses would have to treat customers accordingly to ensure that at the end of the day *avoid this sort of phrase* they keep making the profit that they need and want. Morally however we cannot know if utilitarianism would say that the businesses would have a moral duty as the theory is for the greatest number of people being made happy and therefore in the event of more people being made happy by the mistreatment of customers then the extend of the duty would be low. *Excellent point*

This theory is called the principle of utility. The principle of utility is the idea that the choice that brings about the greatest good for the greatest number is the right choice. *Yes but you are repeating yourself here which actually waters down your argument (by making it feel less rigorous) and wastes time. Surely a paragraph break should follow now??*Another point to consider would be the deontological approach to this duty. Deontological is the focus of the rightness and wrongness of the situation. In the situation of treating customers well would be the right thing to do in a business situation and to treat them badly would be wrong. The teleological approach to this is to come to a conclusion in the situation of what is the right or wrong thing *unclear – why didn't you ground the concept of duty in Kantian ethics and state how a duty might be derived morally?* and so going back to the question utilitarianism would agree that businesses have a moral duty to treat customers well.

In contrast to that Milton Friedman would argue <u>quite the opposite</u>. *Much better to summarise what he does say* Friedman believes that the point of a business is to make money and only money without the consideration of the rights that workers have, the treatment of the workers and the treatment of the customers. *But it may actually be in the interest of greater profit to have a happy and fulfilled workforce* He feels that businesses do not have any social responsibilities however despite these strong beliefs he was not against the idea that businesses should make everyone better off and improve people's lives yet he still believed that the way for this to happen was for businesses to focus on profit alone and everything that was good would follow this principle. *The point Friedman is making is that it is for Parliament (society) to decide the moral boundaries of business activity and for businesses to comply – it isn't for business to work out the morality – their responsibility is to be efficient, profitable, and ensure the survival, growth and prosperity of the organisation.*

On the other hand a strong argument for the duty businesses have is the consideration of the stakeholders and shareholders. A shareholder is someone who has invested money in a business in return for a share of the profits, a stakeholder is a person who is affected by or involved in some form of relationship with a business *shareholders are one type of stakeholder so these two ideas are not exclusive.* Both stakeholders and shareholders are affected by the decisions the company makes. For a shareholder they want to be ensured that they will be getting a profit yet to get this every month or year the business they are giving money to needs to stay a customer favourite in order to keep customers happy to keep their loyalty to the business so that when they do shop the money is going to the company rather than the competition. *Rather a long-winded sentence!* In order to keep the shareholders happy the customers have to be happy which means that they need to be put first and treated well. John lewis is a well known business that believes that customers should be put first and that they have a moral duty towards all of their stakeholders also. *Such as their employees who are fellow owners of the company and get a share of the profits.*

Yet Kantian ethics could argue that businesses are just pretending that they are putting the customers first. A good example to represent this is the shopkeeper example. The shopkeep example is portraying a shopkeeper who pretended to be putting the customers first but he was only doing this to make sure that his shop made a profit. *Kantian ethics should have been properly discussed under the first paragraph on duty, and the idea of motive introduced. You should have shown how Kant might have derived a duty to customers, but also how two duties can easily come into conflict in Kantian ethics. An example might help here: if Trafigura dumps toxic waste in the Ivory Coast as happened in 2011, then profits may be higher, but stakeholders include the local citizens who suffer side effects and illnesses. So a duty of care to citizens there comes into conflict with the duty to maximise profit (which is also a universalisable maxim in the sense that everyone involved with the company would want it to prosper).*

To conclude, I believe that everyone should follow their duties *you haven't shown where these duties come from, or why I should follow a duty and not, say, my own interests or my own pleasure* and do what is morally right yet i believe that this is dependent on the circumstances of a situation. Duties are created by moral laws *no, according to Kant it is a priori reason and universalisability that create moral laws and consistency, which creates the duty to act from a good will* to follow these are our duty. I feel that customers should be the priority to businesses as the customers are keeping that business there is an idea that if everyone obeys certain rules then we will have happier society, but nonetheless, these rules are not absolutes as In Kantian ethics.from going bankrupt and so therefore that business will have a moral obligation to respect their customers. I understand that a key part of every business is to make profit but i do not feel that the treatment of staff and customers needs to be jeopardised for this to happen. I could therefore link my argument to human rights as everyone is equal and we should all be treated the same. *You've tagged on a further idea as an afterthought.*

Total 20/40 50% Grade D

This essay becomes a bit incoherent in places, especially when you introduce the idea of duty as you fail to ground this in any moral theory. The essay needs a clearer contrast between a utilitarian and a Kantian position, and I would use Mill, who is a weak rule utilitarian (meaning he argues for rules which generally we should follow even if these rules can be broken for utilitarian reasons).

AO1 Level 3 (8 marks) A satisfactory demonstration of knowledge and understanding with mostly relevant material. Some accurate knowledge demonstrating understanding through material used but may be lacking in breadth. Sources / academic approaches are used to demonstrate knowledge and understanding with only partial success.

AO2 Level 3 (12 marks) A satisfactory demonstration of analysis and/evaluation in response to the question. Some successful argument. Partially successful analysis and evaluation. Views asserted but often not fully justified. Mostly answers the set question. There is a line of reasoning presented which is mostly relevant and which has some structure.

Assess the view that situation ethics is the most flexible approach to moral decision-making. (19/40 Grade D)

Situation ethics is a theory based around love. It is a teleological theory which means it is a consequential theory and not one based on rules. Situation ethics is not based on all types of love but agapeistic love which is love for your fellow man. In the Christian tradition this may be expressed as, 'Love your neighbour as you love yourself' (Matthew 22:39 The Holy Bible) this making it the most Christian of all theories. A song that was written by Paul McCartney and John Lennon gives the idea of situation ethics "all you need is love".

No need to put 'the Holy Bible' with a reference. Teleological does not mean the same as consequentialist. Consequentialist is about how you weigh the effects of an action so as to determine whether it's good or bad. Teleological means 'linked to final purpose – for example, the purpose here is 'love". You could have a love-based ethic based entirely on non-consequentialist rules. For example, you could argue that exactly following God's commands is the most loving thing to do, because God knows us better than we know ourselves. We want to assess consequences, but we're so bad at it that it would be better for us to follow the rules of a loving God (roughly the Divine Command argument).

Situation Ethics was developed by an Anglican theologian Joseph Fletcher as a result of his critique of Legalism and Antinomianism. Legalism is the idea that there are fixed moral laws which are to be obeyed at all times. Antinomianism is the idea that there are no fixed moral principles but that one acts morally spontaneously. Fletcher was a child of the 60's when free love was seen to be acceptable.

127

"Jesus said nothing about birth control, large or small families, childlessness, homosexuality, masturbation, fornication, premarital intercourse, sterilisation, artificial insemination, abortion, sex, foreplay, petting and courtship. Whether any form of sex (hetero, homo or auto) is good or evil depends on whether love is fully served." (Fletcher)

The precept 'to do whatever is the most loving thing' is not a law but a motive and an attitude that can inform moral choice. One needs to take each situation differently and act in love accordingly even if that means breaking established moral rules/laws. For example, it is considered wrong to steal but if by stealing a gun you are preventing a person from killing people then you have acted in love therefore your theft is non-accountable. In fact the only accountability in Situation Ethics is whether your actions will result in the highest possible expression of love for others (i.e. what is the best decision I can make to help others?).

One of Fletcher's main arguments in 'Situation Ethics' is that Christians are meant to love people, not laws, and it is an argument that is grounded in four working principles and six fundamental principles. These are:

Yes, but the question is 'how is Situation Ethics grounded in these and how do the principles relate to the 'no law' point? You are merely stating rather than establishing the link here.

Four working principles: 1) The practical course of an action is motivated by love; 2) The necessity to always respond in love to each situation; 3) The necessity to accept the premise of acting in love by faith rather than by reason; 4) The desire to put people, not laws, first.

Six fundamental principles: 1) No actions are intrinsically right or wrong. Nothing is good in and of itself except for love. Actions are good if they help people and bad if they don't. One cannot expect to live responsibly with moral absolutes; 2) good actions should not be done for reward (E.g. experiencing a good feeling or seeking altruistic deeds in return) but should be done for their own sake. Jesus and Paul taught love as the highest principle above the Law; 3) Justice is love at work in the community; 4) Love is practical and not selective. We should show love to all, even our enemies. Christian love is unconditional; 5) Love is the end - never a means to something else; 6) Humans have the responsibility of freedom. They are not bound by any Law. With this comes the responsibility to 'do the most loving thing' in every situation.

These types of lists are not really the way to write a good essay. You are simply stating what is contained in Fletcher's book, rather than weaving an analysis/ evaluation around them. Fletcher claims that it is a mistake to generalise. You can't say 'Is it ever right to lie to your family?' The answer must be, 'I don't know, give me an example.' A concrete situation is needed, not a generalisation. 'It all depends' is a well used word by a Situationist. (Vardy & Grosch p.130 Puzzle of Ethics). Many people have noted that situation ethics is very similar to the utilitarian approach except that Fletcher has substituted happiness for love. Yet love is a far harder, and less universal norm than happiness.Possibly only Jesus himself achieve s the agapeic life.

People have many different views on any approach in theology.

Situation Ethics has been criticised on a number of important points. E.g. in order to 'do the most loving thing' in every situation we have to look at the long term consequences of our actions in the present moment. But this is a difficult thing to do. We do not know if our actions will lead to pain or joy but the promotion of love for the Situationist requires us to do so if we are to avoid acting selfishly A good example of this is if an elderly person were to request assisted suicide because it is believed she will otherwise suffer terribly (based on her present illness) or on the other hand she may face up to her responsibilities as a grandmother to her grandchild and stay aliveIt is also possible to act selfishly, in the name of love' without being aware of it (or being very aware of it); some people believe that situation ethics is a very subjective theory and very individualistic. Pope pious had this opinion.

You need to say what Pope Pius said exactly ,and if possible, where he said it. It's worth learning one or two illustrative quotes for each section of the syllabus. They don't need to be long.

Another criticism is, Do murder, lying, cheating and stealing become 'good acts' just because someone commits them in the name of love? There seems to be a confusion here between what is morally good and what is morally right (the act itself - E.g. It may be morally good for me to steal someone's gun to stop them killing people but does that then make stealing morally right?).

Excellent point – which goes to the heart of the ethical debate – is something every intrinsically wrong because of the nature of the act itself? Kant argues there is - it's intrinsically wrong if it cant be universalised or isn't done out of a good will.

Another problem is its lack of rules this means it is up to the person to decide what is right or wrong to do in a situation but people's feelings and emotions do not stay the same what you may think is right one day may have changed by the next. Some believe that you have to have structure in life other wise it does not work.

I think you can bring rules in if you want – as rule utilitarians do – for example, by saying generally keeping your promise is the most loving thing to do.

On the other hand many people believe that situation ethics takes the right approach. It overall shows the most Christian love and it takes into account the complication of life where rules do not change because of some circumstances, and situation ethics may be able to help. It seems to be a practical but flexible theory for people to understand and use as it gives you the freedom within the laws of love. The Agapeic calculus helps offer guide lines to individuals. For Christians it can be the perfect theory as love is at the heart of the morality and supports the teaching of Jesus.

Total Mark 19/40 48% Grade D

AO1 Level 3 (7 marks) A satisfactory demonstration of knowledge and understanding with of mostly relevant material. Some accurate knowledge demonstrating understanding through material used but may be lacking in breadth. Sources / academic approaches are used to demonstrate knowledge and understanding with only partial success

AO2 Level 3 (11 marks) A satisfactory demonstration of analysis and/evaluation in response to the question. Some successful argument. Partially successful analysis and evaluation. Views asserted but often not fully justified. Mostly answers the set question. There is a line of reasoning presented which is mostly relevant and which has some structure.

The last sentence is an afterthought. If it's true then you need to establish this as part of the argument not as an add on. Add-ons usually suggest an underdeveloped thesis. The essay generally promises much more than it delivers and shows how a C or D grade answer could so easily have become a B or A grade with a better strategy. Consider three things: assertions need to be turned into a fuller analysis. For example, the final sentence is an assertion which is never analysed. You might re-read this essay and underline the number of assertions that could have been properly explained. Secondly there needs to be evaluation woven in all the way through. There is little of this. It is more like an apologetic for Fletcher than an analysis/evaluation of Fletcher. Thirdly, never use lists, tempting though it is because you've spent hours learning the four working principles. Instead, try to use examples from these lists to produce a stronger argument. As a final point: Situation ethics is actually one of the hardest ethics to live out, for a number of reasons (difficulty with the idea of agape being perhaps the primary one). It's in this idealism that it parts company with Utilitarianism. It's easy to envisage pleasure, we all experience it, but not so easy to envisage a world run on principles of agapeic love, which is arguably an impossible ideal. Self-interest generally intrudes too much. So we need critical counter-points from other philosophers.

Ethical statements are no more than expressions of emotion. Discuss. (14/40 Grade E)

Ethical statements are statements which contain a moral judgment on something, however, the extent to which moral language can be relied upon is debated. Philosophers such as Ayer, Stevenson, Moore and Ross have addressed the issue of moral language, and the significance of the issue.

Yes, the word is 'prescriptive' – ethical language has a prescriptive 'ought' or 'should' in them. Underlying every question there are sub-issues which you should try and identify in your opening paragraph. The sub-issue in meta-ethics is: is there an objective, naturalistic basis for a moral statement (eg can it be turned into something measurable out there in the real world, or even as an interior experience such as pleasure, as in utilitarian ethics)? Ayer emphatically rejects the naturalistic basis. But is he right to do so?

Emotivist's such as Ayer and Stevenson believe that ethical theories which hold ethical statements are not statements of fact, but are expressions of emotion. ~Therefore would agree with the proposition that ethical statements are no more than expressions of emotion. A.J. Ayer was a British philosopher who studied at the University of Vienna, having graduated from Oxford. He became renowned for his support of logical positivism, and in 1936 he wrote an influential book titled Language, Truth and Logic. In the exam you won't have time for this sort of background information. Building upon the ideas of Wittgenstein and the Vienna Circle, Ayer attempted to set down rules by which language can be judged to see whether it really means anything. You need a paragraph break here. Paragraphs are important for defining units of thought that proceed logically.Ayer believed the main argument of logical positivism was that statements are only meaningful if they fall into one of two categories. It they should be either analytic, or synthetic (verifiable using the senses). An idea he gets from David Hume. Analytic statements are true by definition, we do not have to check whether they are true as they just give us information about what things mean. A dictionary, for example, is full of analytic statements. *This isn't what analytic means here. Analytic means tautological eg like the statement 'all bachelors are unmarried' – the truth of which is contained in the idea of bachelorhood. It makes no sense to say, "John is a bachelor, and here's his wife, Joan!" To a logical positivist an analytic statement is meaningful. Paragraph break needed here as you are now proceeding to a new unit of thought – to do with synthetic statements.* A synthetic statement contains opinion and must be proven true for example, saying 'Fred is allergic to nuts', the statements must be tested to see if that is true. To a logical positivist, in order for a synthetic statement to be meaningful it must be verifiable using empirical evidence, i.e. it has to be possible to test the truth of the statement using experiences available to us. Therefore, if the statement is neither analytic nor empirically verifiable it is meaningless. This style of thinking was in line with that of David Hume, he believed that without abstract reasoning a statement says nothing at all. A statement must be capable of being tested if it is to be proven true of false. This is known as the verification principle.

Yes. Practise structuring your argument – David Hume logically comes first, by about 200 years, not as an afterthought.

C.L. Stevenson was an American philosopher, he developed his thinking in his book Ethics and Language. I believe that most statements were merely emotional expressions, however Stevenson linked this to attitudes. Stevenson argued that moral judgements contain an element that expresses an attitude relative to the fundamental belief of the person in the hope that this will influence others. For example, by saying 'this is good', what a person means is 'I approve this, approve it to'. To Stevenson, moral language is relative to the beliefs that people hold. He believed that moral disagreements are often differences of opinion about what to do, rather than actual disagreements. Emotivism challenges the idea that the term good represents morality, instead it is relativist following the idea that there are no fixed moral laws.

Intuitionists aimed to provide deeper insight into what is meant by the term good and how ethical language can be distinguished. They believe that ethical theories which hold moral statements are part of the natural world no, not in the sense of naturalistic – moral statements are non-naturalistic intuitions and can be recognised or observed, and so would argue against the statement that moral statements are merely an expression of emotion. GE Moore believed that intrinsically good things exist for their own sake, they cannot be analysed, broken down or examined like other things in the physical world. However, they can be recognised. Morality cannot be proven but can be observed. *Known in the sense of 'recognised intuitively' is not quite the same as observing empirically.* Remember Moore introduces the idea of a 'naturalistic fallacy' Moore believed that a person's moral judgements should promote the most goodness, and that is how we can decide what is moral or not. However, Moore rejected the idea of utilitarianism which argued that goodness and happiness can be measured naturalistically for example the hedonic calculus. *Again you are adopting a 'stream of ideas' style which needs proper paragraphing and then linking of the paragraphs back to the question* Moore's theory became known as the naturalistic fallacy. To Moore, good was a simple nation notion, just as yellow as this information ???. You know it when you sit see it. As Animal, such as a horse, is a complex nation *notion* as it can be broken down and observed. Good is good, we know it when we see it. WD Ross built upon the work of Moore, in attempt to understand moral principles one uses when making a moral statement. A person's fundamental principles can often conflict in moral situations, for example, to keep the promise one may have to lie. Other issues also arise, for example different cultures have different principles. It is because of this, Ross argues, that principles should not be taken as absolute values. *Yes, you know by intuition which to take as primary where two goods conflict* Ross, similarly to Moore, believed that goodness is an indefinable term. Moral statements are nearly an expression of our principles. Other ethical theories such as Kantian ethics and utilitarianism also offer moral principles in a similar manner. To avoid the issue of conflicting duties, Ross proposed the idea of prima facie duties. These are moral obligations which we are bound to follow unless there is an overriding obligation. Ross suggested that it is possible to improve our moral knowledge of a situation in order to improve our ability to pass judgement of a situation. Phew! This is a monumentally long paragraph.

In conclusion, emotivism offers a stronger argument regarding ethical language, particularly given the evidence seen through cultural differences in right and wrong. If morality were absolute and observable, we would not see the cultural differences in opinion of ethical behaviour.

14/40 35% Grade E

You need to evaluate emotivism as well as explain it. The evaluation is necessary for the AO2 mark. The same with intuitionism. Is Ayer's theory an adequate view of moral language? Does it allow moral debate to take place? How come most of the great moral theories of the world are naturalistic (natural law, utilitarianism, situation ethics)? Christian ethics accepts the premise that God designed morality into the human mind and also into the natural order and purposes of things.

AO1 Level 3 (7 marks) A satisfactory demonstration of knowledge and understanding with of mostly relevant material. Some accurate knowledge demonstrating understanding through material used but may be lacking in breadth. Sources / academic approaches are used to demonstrate knowledge and understanding with only partial success.

AO2 Level 2   (7 marks) A basic demonstration of analysis and evaluation in response to the question. Only partially answers the question. Some analysis, but not successfully justified. views asserted but with little justification. There is a line of reasoning which has some relevance and which is presented with limited structure.

Note – I am taking the grade boundaries here for the AS exam marked in the summer of 2017, although I know this is a full A level answer. This is pending clarification from the board as to how teachers should assess grades under the new specification. We won't know the grade boundaries until August 2018. The grade boundaries for AS 2017 were:

73% A grade

65% B grade

55% C grade

45% D grade

35% E grade

Is conscience linked to or separate from reason and the unconscious mind? (36/40 Grade A*)

Our conscience is the person's moral sense of right and wrong, and is often viewed as acting as a guide to one's behaviour. The conscience is often thought of being an inner voice inside of us that is created when we are born. *Yes that's one of a number of possibilities, why not say, "for example by Cardinal Newman'?* The idea of conscience - it being either linked to or separate to reason and the unconscious mind - still makes us unique and created in the likeness of God (imago dei). *Who argues this? Mention someone or just refer to the Bible. For example, St Paul speaks of the "Gentiles having a law written on their hearts' (Romans 2:14) which is something close to Aquinas' idea of synderesis* Our conscience also distinguishes us from animals and makes us superior because our reason is practical *guides actions and choices* and judges what is right and wrong. This *is* aspect of conscience is especially important because moral life must be practical, and our ability to reason and make moral judgements connects us to the eternal realm. *Yes* The idea of conscience being linked to or separate to *from* reason and the unconscious mind has been argued by scholars such as psychologists Freud, Philosopher Aquinas and St. Paul. Aquinas's theory emphasis the ideas of synderesis, conscientia, vincible and invincible ignorance. Freud's theory focuses on the idea of id, ego and superego. On the other hand, St Paul describes the human ability to know and choose the good. He taught that all people know what is right and wrong because of our conscience. He said it is written on our hearts, "There is something deep within them that echoes God's yes and no, right and wrong." (Romans 2:14,15, The Message). Overall, I believe Aquinas has the strongest line of argument because he has shown how all humanity can reason right and wrong yet make wrong decisions and as such there is degree of accountability from the person's actions. This means that our conscience is linked to reason and the unconscious mind, however we can chose to override it.

This is rather good as an opening summary – you are pointing the essay in the right direction. However, the paragraph is too long and is trying to say too much. The place of the opening paragraph is to summarise your basic approach and launch your thesis. The thesis is the line or the position you take on the question, whilst also exposing the sub-issues underlying the question. You finally get to the thesis at the end of the paragraph – but I think the lead up to it could be a little more succinct, as I suspect that in the main development of the essay you will be repeating some of this.

Freud was the father of psychoanalysis and had popularised the view than subconscious process are always at work in our minds. Freud talks about *'creates hypothetical categories within the human mind as a framework' is a more analytical and also evaluative way of speaking about Freud – evaluative because it has that word 'hypothetical' suggesting the evaluative idea that 'it cannot be proved'* the id which is classed as a newborn child because they only desire basic needs such as food and sleep. This means that the child's mind is amoral because they don't understand what right or wrong actions are. The id becomes sexually driven whilst breast feeding and then develops their libido (the energy that drives our sexual desires) through maturity. *Good – you might mention the 'pleasure principle' as this connects with utilitarianism in normative ethics* This means that our conscience is not linked to reason because reason is something we are born with rather that it growing through maturity. Furthermore, it also suggests that reason is learnt through maturity rather than being linked to our conscience because we almost have to 'earn it' through experiences and life events.   On the other hand Freud explains that the superego develops as a result of socialisation and growth. This further enforces the fact that our conscience is separate to reason and the unconscious mind because if it was linked it would then mean that we do not have to grow or socialise in order to understand reason. If the superego - this is an aspect of our conscious *life or do you mean conscience here – people tend to confuse the two* - needs to develop through socialisation *parental praise and blame – make the link to conscience clear* and growth it then shows we are not born with it, therefore, people will have different superego's because some people socialise more while others don't. Our conscious is something everyone is born with, we all have the same, it is innate.

Synoptic point: you can link Freud's idea of the id and the ego to Plato's charioteer trying to control twin forces of passion and spirit (emotion). The superego isn't quite the same as Plato's reason, but the mature conscience in Freud (when the inner hidden sources of guilt and shame are exposed) is I think close to Plato's idea of regulating reason. I like the use of the link word 'furthermore' which suggest analytical writing. Surprisingly few students make use of this word.

In addition, St Paul strengthens the argument that our conscience is linked to reason and the unconscious mind because in 2 Corinthians 1:12 he says "God has given us our conscience" and "Our conscience is not created through things we have learnt". This is a strength because it shows that our conscience is linked to reason and the unconscious mind because we are born with it because we are made in the image of God, therefore it is not learnt through experiences unlike Freud's theory. *You could also link Paul's view in Romans 2:14-16 to natural law theory eg Aquinas' use of synderesis (as mentioned in the opening comments I made in red)...the Gentiles (ie non-Jews) too have the natural law 'written on their hearts' says St Paul..*

On the other hand, *good, this phrase suggest a contrasting line of thought, hence hinting at analysis and also (perhaps) evaluation to come.* Freud's id theory does suggest that our conscience is linked to our unconscious mind because we are born with sexual desires, even at the age of 3-6 years - the phallic stage.

141

Although Freud suggests we are, there is limited scientific evidence to support this theory. *Yes. I'm not sure there is any evidence at all for this! Of course if you an make reference to any that would be good...or to an academic who criticises Freud for this then that would also fortify the argument here.* On the basis *assumption* that it is true, then there is an aspect of our conscience being linked to our unconscious mind because we have an innate understanding of sexual desires because we are born with them. The reason it is linked to our unconscious mind is because it's something we do without knowing we are doing it, for example our conscience is not a verbal voice that tells us to give to charity. Freud believes that as humans our conscience is linked to reason and our unconscious mind because children have physical, emotional and sexual needs. This links into Freud's explanation of the Oedipus Complex, his notion was taken from the Greek legend Oedipus and explains that all boys want to kill their fathers and sleep with their mothers.

Good clear writing. But why not add a comment of evaluation as you go along? For example, Freud imposes a hypothesis on our mental activity which is impossible to prove – it's a way of looking at the mind which may contain important insights but also has deficiencies – simply as an empirical fact few of us seem to hate our fathers in the way suggested.

In contrast to this, *good link phrase* many other psychologist, scientist and philosophers would disagree with Freud because his theory of the Oedipus Complex has been disputed due to the very little *scientific (empirical)* basis for his theories. The experimental basis for Freud was limited because his largely female patients were not typical of the whole of society because they were rich Victorians. Furthermore, his idea of children having sexual desires during very young infant years has been viewed upon as strange because at the age of 3-6 most young children are unaware of anything sexual and do not have sexual desires that is linked to the unconscious mind and reason. It is a disturbing complex to accept because the thought of children being sexually driven through their conscience is alarming for many. Furthermore, it also suggests that our conscience is not linked to reason and our unconscious mind because very very few boys fulfil this desire to kill their fathers and sleep with their mothers.

Excellent mix of analysis and evaluation in this paragraph. As an exercise, take this paragraph and highlight the evaluative comments. Remember – evaluation points out something that's good/bad about something else, or in arguments, what is weak or strong about an argument. A good strategy is to take an author who disagrees with a certain point of view and bounce your comments off their argument.

Alternatively Aquinas believes that to understand conscience you must understand ratio - practical reason. Therefore, they must be linked to reason and the unconscious mind because they work as one component. Our ratio is a fundamental part of being a human and distinguishes human beings from other animals because it is a divine gift from God which allows us to chose moral actions. Therefore, this means that our conscience is linked to reason because it is placed in every person as a result of being created by God (imago dei). This reason is the practical sort which allows us to judge what is right or wrong. We have the unconscious mind of think what should be done and can be done by the agent. *This sentence makes no sense – even in the exam it's always a good idea to give your work a quick read through. The best time to do this is just before writing the last paragraph – just to check you haven't strayed off the question.* Ratio implies for Aquinas that human beings are capable of reasoning on a number of levels – both a priori and a posteriori. It allows him to argue that the image of God is distinctive – it means for example, that whilst we share some elements with the animal world (eg desire to survive and to reproduce) there are other elements unique to human beings – the ability and desire to worship God, appreciate beauty and create social rules which are the basis for morality.

Aquinas put forward the idea of 'synderesis' which means humans have good habit or right reason because God implanted direction towards good and away from evil. *Yes – it's a teleological orientation for Aquinas which we observe a posteriori (by experience)* Synderesis and sensuality are within mankind, however human beings are capable of leaning towards the food *good* and away from selfishness because our conscience is wired that way. Synderesis is a habit of learning *action?* and humans can use ratio to refine the habit of synderesis. Here, we can see it has a small similarity to Freud's understanding that our superego needs to socialise and grow because synderesis also states that it's a habit of learning rather than it being an innate understanding.

Moreover, Aquinas also talks about the vincible and invincible ignorance. Here, Aquinas is clear that our conscience is binding, even when it is mistaken because reason may be incomplete because of the confusion between real and apparent goods (evil deeds). *Always explain when you state – and here you haven' explained what the 'confusion between real and apparent goods' actually is.* Vincible ignorance is a lack of knowledge for which a person can be held responsible because they should have known better. A person might fail to educate themselves without the necessary knowledge which means they deserved to get blamed because they should've known. This means that our conscience and reason is separate because it can be argued that our conscience can led us to make moral decisions and our reason can also result us into making alternative decisions, rather than working together.

Example might help eg if I shoot into a wood without checking there's no-one there, I am guilty of vincible ignorance if I kill someone. UK law calls this culpable negligence.

On the other hand, invincible ignorance is a lack of knowledge for which a person is not responsible because the person acts out of their best knowledge. However, they still get it wrong; although this is still immoral God will condemn humans for this. This means that our conscience is linked to our reason because we made a moral choice by using both our conscience and reason however, the only reason it wasn't moral was because we were prohibited the full amount of information. *Good – you are relating this back to the question set.*

In conclusion, we can see that there are elements of both Aquinas and Freud's theory that support the ideas of our conscience being both linked and separate to reason and the unconscious mind. Both theories talk about how conscience is made from experiences that come later on in life. In has been established that Aquinas has the strongest line of argument because he has explained humanity can reason right and wrong due to our conscience being linked to reason however, we can still choose to override it our of choice or being deprived from the full amount of knowledge.

Mark 36/40 Grade A (90%)*

Excellent answer – A writing and showing plenty of analysis, evaluation, technical language, use of good linkage words and phrases, and a powerful line of argument. Notice how the main thesis is presented in the opening paragraph which also sets out the boundaries to the territory the question will explore. We need to practise imposing these boundaries for two reasons. The first is because exam questions are open-ended and have a sub-agenda implicit in them which needs to be thought out. The second is that it stops us wandering around in our answer – in other words, producing a generalised answer to a general question is a mistake. You need to provide a specific answer to a question whose generality has been brought down to specifics. In essence, this is frequently the difference between an A grade student and someone who fails to achieve A grade. It is a difference of analytical and evaluative skill not of knowledge.*

Level 6 AO1 (15 marks)

An excellent attempt to address the question showing understanding and engagement with the material; excellent ability to select and deploy relevant information. Extensive range of scholarly views, academic approaches, and/or sources of wisdom and authority are used to demonstrate knowledge and understanding

Level 6 AO2 (21 marks)

An excellent demonstration of analysis and evaluation in response to the question.Confident and insightful critical analysis and detailed evaluation of the issue. Views skilfully and clearly stated, coherently developed and justified. Excellent line of reasoning, well-developed and sustained, which is coherent, relevant and logically structured.

'Conscience is the voice of God working within us.' Discuss. (33/40 Grade A)

Philosophers and psychologists alike are divided on their understanding of conscience. For some, like Aquinas, it's a God-given faculty which enables us (through right reason) to act morally, for others it's the literal 'voice of God' acting within us, whilst for Freud it's merely the internalised values of *parents or* society, adopted from figures of authority. There are certainly strengths and weaknesses to each of these positions, particularly with regards to whether they can be verified empirically or not, and the ways in which they result in different outcomes for different people. Arguably though, modern approaches from psychology are able to withstand the greatest scrutiny.

Very clear thesis and evaluative line are introduced here from the start. The opening paragraph is crucial because it launches the essay in the right direction and promises much. You can almost grade many essays on the opening paragraph – and it might be an interesting exercise to try.

The belief that conscience is the literal, objective 'voice of God' working within us is a markedly intuitionist one. In other words, we should be able to listen to our conscience and spontaneously 'intuit' the right course of action, reaching a consensus on what it's telling us. For the 18th-Century, Anglican theologian Butler, conscience holds the preeminent position within human decision-making, as it 'magisterially exerts itself … without being consulted.' Therefore, (being authoritative/automatic,) he believed it should reign supreme among our moral authorities, governing every moral decision we face. So highly did Butler think of conscience, that he claimed it was the distinguishing feature of the human condition, granting us a status superior to that of other animals. Likewise, 19th-Century theologian Cardinal Newman argued that when an individual follows their conscience, they are simultaneously following the divine law. He described it as the 'messenger of God,' something more than just a 'law of the mind,' which intuitively directs our moral decision-making. Most notably, St. Augustine also believed Conscience could be identified as the 'voice of God.' He argued that when we adhere to its suggestions, we are following the word of God, a word that implicitly tells us right from wrong. As with Butler and Newman, this conception of Conscience is described in quite abstract, metaphysical terms. In particular, as an 'illumination of the soul,' and as a personal revelation by God.

This paragraph is a bit too dense and should have been split. That said, there's a lot of good material here. I don't think you need to introduce so many different authors because, in the process, you can fail to say anything very interesting about any of them. I can see the essential point here but as a comment there is no appreciation of just how different Newman and Butler are (neither appear in the new spec but it is essential to introduce counter-arguments from somewhere, so why not keep using them?)

In reality, this is a far cry from how conscience seems to work, at least anecdotally-speaking. Disagreements concerning ethics between different Christian sects and schools of thought should be evidence enough that the 'voice of God' is not infallible, or at least that conscience is difficult to read and interpret. For example, one Christian's 'conscience' might tell them that abortion is morally reprehensible because it involves the taking of a life, however soon after conception. Whereas, for another Christian, conscience might direct them towards a more liberal, 'pro-choice' approach, if it's determined that this would benefit the health and wellbeing of the mother. Even if both are steeped in the same Christian tradition: are well-versed in scripture, are regular attendants of their local Church, and so on, different conclusions (supposedly derived from conscience) could be reached. Taking this discrepancy into account, there are two obvious ways for the intuitionist to respond. Either conscience is not the voice of God working within us, the more difficult concession to make, or the voice of God is so unclear that it causes people to behave in different ways, regardless of the likeness of their upbringings. If the latter response is made though, there'd surely be little purpose in following conscience at all (i.e. because of its stifling ambiguity). Likewise, these claims fall a long way short of satisfying the 'verification' and 'falsification' principles - in that they have no grounding in empirical/sense-experience evidence and don't appear to correspond to any agreed reality.

In many ways, this model fails to reflect the flexible/malleable nature of Conscience and is too idealistic. 'Ideally,' being able to hear the 'voice of God working within us' would negate all of the difficulties of moral decision-making. *Surely the phrase 'voice of God' is actually a metaphor anyway – there are no words literally appearing in someone's head (usually).* The Christian ethicist could sleep-easy knowing that their torture of the terrorist was justified; saving lives by revealing the location of the timebomb. Or that their support of Peter Sutcliffe's serial killings 'because his conscience told him to do so' is well-supported by Christian theological thought (i.e. that Conscience is the infallible voice of God working within us).

I think these long paragraphs need splitting up into smaller, more coherent units. This is essential when you have just 40 minutes because there is a limit to what can be said. I encourage you to practice thesis statements leading to a five paragraph structure and then an eight paragraph (maximum) structure where the essential point of each of the main a paragraph's is turned into two paragraphs with suitable linkages (such as 'however' for a contrasting point).

An approach to conscience which is similar, but contrasting in the nuanced way it treats the Conscience's provenance differently from Butler, Newman and Augustine, is that of Aquinas. Taking inspiration from the works of Aristotle, he argued that conscience exists in the understanding of rational, immutable moral principles, and the way in which these are derived from the relationship between ratio, synderesis and conscientia. That is, Conscience comes from God in so far as He instilled in us the faculty of reason, to work out his divine law and be able to apply it in making moral judgements. Ratio is the ability to understand our conscience through the use of 'right' reason. It is more than mere comprehension, and has some 'progressive' element to it - in making moral decisions, the moral agent's thinking is moved from one state to another. Synderesis then, is the habit of humans to do good and shun evil, through the application of this 'ratio.' Aquinas believed that this habit could be cultivated through consistent moral righteousness (e.g. a 'golden mean',) and in so doing, become a leaning/inclination which is easier to apply. Finally, conscientia describes the acts arising from knowledge, gained through applying ratio to synderesis - 'a pronouncement of the mind.' This overcomes some of the contentions with the first position - that Conscience is the literal 'voice of God' working within us. In particular, the criticism that if Conscience has objective origins, it shouldn't direct people towards different decisions. To use the prior example, the discrepancy in applying Conscience to decide whether abortion is morally reprehensible or not.

The Thomist would have no such qualms. They could argue that the difference in opinion comes from an imbalance of ratio, synderesis and conscientia. *Yes this is the key distinction in Aquinas giving his theory a 'both…and' feel* Perhaps immorality of the past has corrupted their sense of synderesis, and they are no longer inclined to act morally, but instead to lean towards choices which 'do evil and shun good' (e.g. having a pro-choice attitude). Or perhaps they have an inferior faculty of reason (e.g. as a result of mental illness,) meaning that they cannot combine introspection and rationality to work out what is moral and what isn't. conscience can be misled or misinformed, as it's not reliant on the infallible voice of God, but on the human faculty of reason. Therefore, its decisions can be doubted, and it can result in morally dubious outcomes. Another strength of Aquinas' position is that it doesn't exclude morality for the non-believer. It's equally possible for the atheist to use their faculty of reason to arrive at moral conclusions as it is for the theist - the only difference being their belief regarding the provenance of this faculty. Indeed, this view is also compatible with more secular understandings of conscience, as it has some element of 'learning' to it, and is not assumed to be innate from birth. Instead, synderesis must be cultivated through repeated use of 'right reason,' and so the Conscience develops as the individual develops (i.e. in accordance with modern psychology). Hence, it can be argued that Aquinas' understanding of conscience is the most compelling of those which take it to be 'God-given' in some way. However secular arguments, from modern psychology, are more defensible still.

These two paragraphs present a very subtle and excellent discussion of ratio, synderesis and conscientia.

One noteworthy proponent of this secular view of conscience is the psychologist Sigmund Freud. For Freud, there is neither a soul nor any moral absolutes. Instead, our values are the product of our upbringing, and conscience is merely a construct - the relationship between one's primal desires and the messages given to them from figures of moral authority (e.g. a clergyman, teacher or parent). In order to understand this position, it is important to first understand Freud's beliefs about the mind, and the way it operates at different levels of consciousness. At the deepest level, is the unconscious mind, domain of our repressed thoughts, feelings and desires in their most primitive forms. Above this, is the preconscious mind, home to memories which are not readily available but accessible when called upon. Most superficially, is the conscious mind, where the thoughts a person currently has exist, and a part of our psyche which the unconscious mind cannot access.

Within these different levels of the mind exist the three parts of our 'psychic apparatus': the id, the ego and the superego - which are fundamentally intertwined, and which develop at different stages of upbringing. The id is the entirely unconscious part of our personality that exists from birth. It follows a primitive 'pleasure principle,' acting chaotically according to our inclinations and desires. The ego is the part of our personality which mediates the relationship between our primitive desires (i.e. the id) and compliance with social norms. Instead of a 'pleasure principle,' it is driven by a 'reality principle' which reconciles the ego and the id - keeping our actions 'in check.' This operates at the conscious and preconscious levels of the mind. Freud describes the id and the ego by way of analogy, comparing them to a rider and their horse. With the rider (ego) being responsible for keeping the horse (id) under control. The last part of the human psyche to develop is the superego, the repository of the internalised moral standards of society, and the values instilled in us by figures of authority. It exerts a feeling of guilt when these values/standards are rejected and operates at every level of the mind. Together, these levels of the mind and the psyches which develop within them make up the conscience. So in many ways, Freud's conscience is neither rationalist, or intuitionist. Instead, it can be described as 'pre-rational,' the inevitable mental conflict between the primitive desires that our id wills us towards, and the restraint that the ego and superego (with its accompanying sense of guilt) place on these desires.

Freud's theory forms a very compelling argument *one or two evaluative comments might have been inserted here.* that suggests conscience is 'learnt,' developed through our upbringing and the figures that influence it. It explains the inconsistencies between different peoples' sense of morality whilst still being applicable to the believer and the non-believer alike. Even if our morality is 'heteronomous,' subservient to figures of authority, we can still allow for this authority to be God. Or more widely, religious institutions (such as the Roman Catholic Church). This perspective is not even contingent on the existence of God. For an authority that exists behind a veil is the same as an authority that exists in front of one. An authority that exists merely as text is the same as an authority that exists in speech. And an authority that exists in fantasy is the same as an authority that exists in reality, so far as the individual and their behaviour is concerned. Therefore, it's difficult to hold that conscience is the voice of God working within us, but Conscience may well be the perceived authority of God acting upon us.

Total 33/40 82% Grade A

Excellent essay in parts. Notice the strength of the conclusion and some of the deep insights within the essay. There is a strong contrast between Freud and Aquinas and a very detailed evaluation of Aquinas. These ideas are linked to other more synoptic ideas such as intuitions and intuitionism in ethics, or the idea of design in philosophy of religion. However, there is a problem in the style of writing. The student doesn't really understand how to paragraph for maximum effect and would need to practise tightening up the argument by paragraphing more effectively, and then linking the paragraphs together with analytical words and phrases (see the appendix at the back of the book for a full list of these). Sometimes you can try to do and say too much – and the brighter you are, the more you may suffer from this problem. Be brutal. Pare it down. Go for strength and logic over length and you can achieve full marks. The essay slightly falls down because in trying to say too much - the evaluation and development in the paragraph on 'the voice of God' is rather generalised. Another example: there is very little evaluation of Freud in the paragraph near the end of the essay.

AO1 Level 6 (14 marks) An excellent attempt to address the question showing understanding and engagement with the material; excellent ability to select and deploy relevant information. Extensive range of scholarly views, academic approaches, and/or sources of wisdom and authority are used to demonstrate knowledge and understanding.

AO2 Level 5 (19 marks) A very good demonstration of analysis and evaluation in response to the question. successful and clear analysis, evaluation and argument. Views very well stated, coherently developed and justified. There is a well–developed and sustained line of reasoning which is coherent, relevant and logically structured.

'Is the conscience rational?' (28/40 Grade B)

The idea of the conscience, widely defined as 'our moral sense of right and wrong', is central to the ethical decision making process, its origins as either a rational, learned or innate sense widely changing the nature of our resulting decisions. St Augustine understood the conscience to be the voice of God directly communicating with the individual, a stance I will reveal as flawed throughout this essay due to its damning moral and practical implications alongside the general incompatibility of the argument. Sigmund Freud proposed a contrary approach, deeming the conscience to be a product of environmental factors driven by guilt, a position equally faulty due to its demotion of humanity to mere machines, our morality at the mercy of outside causes. It was Thomas Aquinas who argued for the notion of a conscience driven by reason, an argument I will support due our human experience of autonomous decision alongside the emphasis placed on the moral agent.

Excellent example of how to launch an essay clearly. Notice that the candidate uses the personal pronoun 'I' which despite what many teachers believe, is absolutely fine as long as you don't overdo it. Philosophers use "I' all the time, usually because they want to own an original idea or a thesis.

The early theologian Saint Augustine, a key proponent of the Christian concept of conscience, understood it to be a divine faculty, the direct voice of God communicating his will to the individual. He asserted the conscience as a innate, physical entity, alluding to its physicality within the world in his words taken from 'Confessions', "Did the chaste dignity of conscience appear to me". Through Augustine's presentation of the conscience as a God-given tool by which we can observe his will, the human ability to reason is made void, instead demoting us to vehicles of God's will. The implication of the theory is that the conscience is fully authoritative, and should thus be followed unquestioningly, generating heavy moral implications if the conscience is ill-advised or mistaken.

Are we then to follow our conscience even if we deduce it to be wrong through the powers of reason? Those who commit indefensible acts such as the 9/11 plane hijacking often claim they were following their God-given conscience, a claim which does not change the immorality of their act. Did God support this horrendous crime? Through this, Augustine's approach leads to two unsatisfactory outcomes, either God is evil (and thus should not be followed), or he is simply not the source of the conscience, undermining the entirety of the argument. This crucial pitfall in Augustine's approach implies the need for a conscience driven by reason, something greater than merely an inside voice, a thought echoed in the words of Thomas Aquinas taken from his 'Summa Theologica', "Conscience is reason making right decisions and not a voice giving us commands". Through the transference of our autonomous powers over to an external agent, moral decisions of the individual lose all value, a dysfunctional and mechanistic system which degrades the worth of the moral agent whilst removing all moral accountability.

Good use of rhetorical questions here to probe an argument critically.

Freud promoted the idea of a learned conscience, one driven by guilt. His ideas about the conscience are based on his beliefs regarding the development of the mind, initially distinguishing between the 'id', driven by our desires, and the 'ego', the rational self, which generates a practical awareness of reality. The 'superego' develops through the internalised voices of others from the age of 5, reflecting guilt and pleasure stemming from reactions to approval and disapproval, ultimately reducing our morality to the most simple of pleasure pain reactions. As the 'superego' develops it becomes an inseparable part of the individual, irrespective of rational thought due to its innate *wrong word to use here as innate means we are born with it - whereas Freud is arguing that conscience develops in early childhood*, guilt based nature, forming the very essence of who we are.

This is a concise summary fo Freud's position but I would bring out how Freudian theory is conscience in conflict as each element is in a sense working against the other - producing neurosis.

Due to the nature of the conscience as an irrational part of the subconscious mind, the autonomy of the individual is made obsolete, removing the notion of moral responsibility entirely. This reductionist view of human agency is damning on both a practical and moral level, generating an entirely relative approach to ethics through lack of moral responsibility. While I acknowledge the impact of childhood influences on our morality, I would dispute the claim that these influences have the ability to form the entirety of our conscience or have the ultimate power to control our decisions. Freud's theory implies, for example, that if one was brought up in Nazi Germany, with the possibility of punishment for going against the regime, the individual's conscience would be inseparably linked with the nazi mindset, a sentiment shown to be untrue by the numbers who rebelled against the nazis despite internalised feelings of shame for doing so. It would be wrong to imply we are machines being blindly driven by the subconscious wills of our mind.

Thomas Aquinas proposed a conscience driven by reason, a rational faculty which enables us to choose right from wrong ("The faculty of reason making moral decisions"). He argued that moral decision making requires synderesis, the principle to 'doing good and avoiding evil' combined with conscientia, the "application of knowledge to activity", in which we must use our power of reason to distinguish good from evil, a concept in keeping with Aristotle's 'phronesis'. As opposed to the learned conscience proposed by Freud, or the innate conscience proposed by the Church, Aquinas' notion of conscience

157

stands in keeping with the idea of 'moral judgement', in which practical reason must be exercised in order to decide upon the best course of action. While our synderesis is an innate tool, given by God, the conscientia is a moral skill acquired over time, with the ultimate end of acting morally. Thus, the conscience is equated with our rational capacity to reason, a capacity Aquinas held as of the utmost importance ("To disparage the dictate of reason is equivalent to condemning the command of God").

You need to evaluate as you go along, paragraph by paragraph - this essay is becoming too descriptive.

Aquinas' view of the conscience as a rational tool is one that relates to the role of the individual as moral agent, a position which should be treated as of the utmost importance. To attribute the conscience to anything other than our own reason is to embrace a morality we are not in control of, a highly problematic stance which, through relinquishing the role of the autonomous agent makes morality itself void, initiating a society of complete moral dysfunction.

Mark 28/40 (70%) Grade B

AO1 Level 5 (12 marks) A very good attempt to address the question demonstrating knowledge and understanding. Very good selection of relevant material, technical terms mostly accurate. a very good range of scholarly views, academic approaches, and/or sources of wisdom and authority are used to demonstrate knowledge and understanding.

AO2 Level 4 (16 marks) A good demonstration of analysis and evaluation in response to the question. Generally successful analysis, evaluation and argument. Views well stated, with some development and justification. Answers the question set well. There is a well–developed line of reasoning which is clear, relevant and logically structured. But more evaluation needs to be interwoven and contrasting viewpoints made explicit.

This is a good example of an essay that just falls off an A grade for three reasons. First, there is not enough evaluation as the essay goes along. Secondly the analysis is a little bit too descriptive. For example, we need a bit more discussion of synderesis and it could be pointed out how synderesis, as the image of God in us orientating us towards good ends, is fundamentally opposed by evangelical Christians who argue we are 'sold into sin' and 'do the very things we hate' (St Paul, Romans 7). Thirdly we need a stronger contrast between the two conflicting views (or even the three views in the very good opening paragraph). I would also like to see some additional authors mentioned - for example, Keith Ward's criticisms of Freud as reductionist. To conclude - the essay has some very good elements, and the student writes well. It does not however move into level 6 excellence, apart from the first paragraph.

Critically assess the view that natural law is the best approach to issues surrounding sexual ethics. (38/40 Grade A*)

I have set this title as an exercise in which the maximum number of words is 1000, to try to encourage students to write less of better quality. I have also asked that this student unpacks the essay title fully in the opening paragraph and identifies a clear line of reasoning. The essay is not intended to be the only approach or even a perfect answer – but it does achieve A* and students are asking me what an A* answer looks like.

Natural Law as developed by Thomas Aquinas attempted to reconcile the Greek teleological wordlview with Christianity, where teleology requires the true purpose (telos) of human beings to be clearly defined. This purpose is designed into us by God. The issue here is – how do we unpack issues around pre-marital sex or homosexual behaviour in order to gain moral guidance on right and wrong, and when contrasted say with utilitarian ethics, does natural law create a pathway that is in some sense better or clearer for the individual? My argument here is that natural law as interpreted by Aquinas is often misunderstood, and when placed in its proper context suggests a superior way of deciding on sexual ethical behaviour than utilitarianism.

Your opening paragraph is very clear and has provided a clear line on the question above. At A level you need to narrow questions down to make them manageable. Here you narrow in two ways. You provide a simple contrast between two ethical theories in order to decide which is 'best'. You can't take every ethical theory in 40 minutes. And secondly, you provide two examples of sexual ethics – pre-marital sex and homosexuality. It's good to take the second because the attitude to homosexual behaviour is one where natural law theorists in the Roman Catholic church have taken the strongest line. And it will be good to see if you can evaluate this line clearly and persuasively. One small point – natural law has both deontological and teleological aspects – deontological, in the sense of it being 'law' and teleological because as you mention, it's based on true purpose.

The proper context for Aquinas' theory is Aristotelean ethics. For Aristotle, the final cause defines the true purpose of any thing, and this applies to humans as well. The true purpose is for human beings to reason well, to gain wisdom by reflecting on experience and to head towards Eudaimonia – a state of human flourishing or fulfilment in which we become the best person that we can be. This is a lifetime quest – as Aristotle reminds us 'one swallow doesn't make a spring". Human beings need to orientate themselves towards these rational purposes. Then both personal and social good is established and developed.

Concise and clear with a relevant and accurate quote.

Aquinas takes this teleological worldview and works it around Christian themes of the revelation of God in the natural world. The glory of God is manifest in the design of human beings. We have, says Aquinas synderesis designed into us – and it means we are all born with a natural orientation towards good ends. These good ends are general primary precepts which include such things as preservation of life, reproduction, and living in society. It is therefore under the reproductive and social ends that sexual ethics falls. This is why, in interpreting this and applying thisto actual life, we find natural law arguing for one human nature which is heterosexual. This is why Humane Vitae states that homosexuality is 'intrinsically disordered' because in Catholic theology it represents behaviour against the natural heterosexual precept of reproduction.

Good synoptic link to the design argument in the Philosophy of Religion paper. Synderesis is correctly identified as the starting point – Aquinas calls it the 'first principle of the natural law' because it applies to Christian and to atheist alike. We all are designed to head towards good goals.

Utilitarian ethics does not share this pre-occupation with an idealised form of human nature. It is true, however that there is a theory of rationality here: utilitarians seek to maximise happiness for the maximum number employing a reasoned calculation (either using a hedonic calculus, as in Bentham, or a more subtle calculation of personal and social benefit as In Mill). When combined with Mill's harm principle we can say that as far as homosexuality is concerned we can maximise our own pleasure as long as we don't produce harm for others. It is pleasure, but pleasure applied to a social context of other people's response and experience.

I like the emphasis on different rationalities – the utilitarian rationality is actually empirical and they are trying to bring science to bear on ethics. The harm principle comes in Mill's essay On Liberty but it is a good strategy to integrate it with his utilitarianism.

So, taking pre-marital sex, we find, as Peter Vardy has argued that the utilitarian scales have tipped with various changes in contraceptive practice, eliminating risks of disease or pregnancy and also with the dismantling of taboos about sex which had in the past produced pain (or shame) attached to sleeping with someone before marriage. However we straightaway encounter two problems here. One is that we tend to take the lower bodily pleasure of sex and ignore higher spiritual values which may be implied by sexual conduct. For example, it might be argued that promiscuous pleasure seeking pre-marital sex has harmful personal and social consequences. In the longer term, it may produce a sense of the individual being of little worth, or merely a pleasure machine.

Good evaluative point here. I like the introduction of the negative disutility of social taboos.

Perhaps this is why the Roman Catholic Church emphasises two natural law functions for sex: the unitive and procreative. The unitive means human beings bond spiritually by sex, and particularly promiscuous sex does not create human bonding of this kind. Secondly, if sex is about procreation then the Catholic view is that contraception is immoral – it interferes with the true God-given purpose. My argument though is different. I believe natural law is presented as over restrictive in Catholic theology because of the concern about relativism. Natural law is presented as more hard line in its rules than it need Natural law isn't inherently anti-pleasure either.

Interesting point although you don't really explain why natural law isn't anti-pleasure when the precepts don't seem to include pleasure as part of them.

Secondary principles, which are approximate conclusions of the general precepts, do not have to be this hard and non-negotiable. For example, there may be social benefits from having a softer line on pre-marital sex – as it helps human beings grow into the idea of a sexual relationship by experience. Also contraception allows for a moderation in population growth and the elimination of disease – so strengthening the precept of living in society and growing the idea of social good. Arguably the very rigidity of Catholic teaching is counter-productive and fails to give us guidelines of what to do when two moral goods (saving life versus reproduction) come into conflict as seems to be the case in Africa.

I like the way you discuss the precepts in the light of an applied example here – very good.

To conclude then, natural law as reinterpreted in the light of Aquinas' theory (and against catholic interpretations) is actually superior to utilitarianism, as it manages to provide a broader objective basis for moral decision making, the basis of the personal and social life, compared with the narrow and rather body-feelings focus of utilitarian pleasure. And with the 'intrinsic disorder' of homosexuality, we simply need to recognise that the assumption of one rational nature is false – a move which does not undermine the basic for of reasoning in natural law. Catholic reasoning suggest a harder deontology than the Greek teleological worldview, as developed by Aquinas himself, actually permits.

TOTAL 38/40 Grade A*

Nicely rounded up into a strong and very interesting conclusion. The overall thrust of this argument is successfully and clearly stated – and the applied issues are identified in sufficient detail to convince the examiner that the question is being fully engaged with. The points made are frequently subtle and go beyond the normal standard of textbook regurgitation. In other words, it is reflective answer and deserves a very high mark showing excellent understanding and development of an analytical and evaluative line.

AO1 Level 6 (15 marks) An excellent attempt to address the question showing understanding and engagement with the material; excellent ability to select and deploy relevant information. Extensive range of scholarly views, academic approaches, and/or sources of wisdom and authority are used to demonstrate knowledge and understanding.

AO2 Level 6 (23 marks) An excellent demonstration of analysis and evaluation in response to the question. Confident and insightful critical analysis and detailed evaluation of the issue. Views skilfully and clearly stated, coherently developed and justified. Excellent line of reasoning, well-developed, sustained, and coherent, relevant and logically structured.

Christian Thought (H573/3)

The Christian Thought paper takes some snapshots in the history of Christian Theology in order to answer some basic questions, such as 'what do we understand by human nature?", "how is Jesus perceived in history and today?", and "how has modern culture shaped belief?".

If we also bear in mind that we are developing and practising skills that help us to read our own culture, then I think we will find this paper very stimulating.

The word that is missing form the syllabus (but which unites the whole syllabus) is *hermeneutics.* Hermeneutics is the study of interpretation. Feminists, for example, adopt a *hermeneutics of suspicion* - they argue that the Bible is riddled with patriarchal ideas which are then developed in Church history to maintain an unequal status for women. Marxist and liberation theologians adopt a *critical hermeneutic* which sees class interest present in our interpretation, an idea echoed by Feud in the Future of an Illusion who gives a close analysis of how Christianity has been used to keep oppressed people from rebellion.

Interestingly, some argue that Jesus is no longer of interest to students. I disagree with this view. I think it is the way Jesus is presented by organised religion and by textbooks which turns people off, as Jesus of the New Testament is a profoundly subversive figure, who we may well have domesticated and made safe. I think students could do well to reconnect with the original Jesus. One writer who will help you do this is Ched Myers, whose interpretation of Mark's gospel in his book *Binding the Strong Man* is truly revolutionary.

Finally Dietrich Bonhoeffer provides us with a case study of courageous action and a situational approach to ethics, which combines with an interpretation of

Jesus as a moral example to us all. Moreover, if our culture has indeed destroyed the idea of agape love, and failed in a sense to learn the lessons of the Holocaust, then this is an excellent place to start if we are to re-evaluate our own lives, and redirect them in a more worthwhile, less self-centred direction. The Holocaust in a sense changed everything, including theology. It was the ultimate evil and affront to us all.

'The Church should decide what is morally good'. Discuss. (36/40 A*)

Christians have differing opinions on the source of morality. While the Catholic Church has in the past claimed to be central to ethics in the Christian community, this has been challenged both by Catholics like Hans Kung and Protestants such as John Calvin who believe morality cannot be perfectly derived by the Church. Dietrich Bonhoeffer has also sought to show how granting moral power to the Church can lead to immoral outcomes. Personally, I believe that while the Church is important to society in deciding what is morally good allowing it to be the only moral authority in society grants it too much authority and could even lead to the Church and society becoming debased and corrupt.

Very good introduction that addresses the question directly. Scholars and divergent views are signposted, giving a confident start and the candidate signposts their own view signally the start of what should hopefully be a well-developed line of reasoning.

Few Christians believe that the Church is the only genuine moral authority, as true morality is generally believed to be revealed through revelation. However the view that morality is best worked out by the Church is much more common. The heteronomous view that reason, the Bible, and the Church all work in conjunction to reveal what is morally good is held by the Magisterium of the Catholic Church. They argue in the Catechism that clergymen's theological education and centuries of Church precedent allow it to be the 'pillar and bulwark of truth' and by extension the Church is best placed to decide what is morally good. While this seems coherent, it does not take into account how the Church's past decisions have in cases been immoral. The sale of indulgences was agreed to be simoniacal by Church councils in the 16th century and against

169

canon law, and yet they were sold for centuries prior, with the Church doing nothing to stop it. Clearly a focus on Church-derived morality will not always result in the most moral outcome.

A confident paragraph showing strength in knowledge and understanding of the heteronomous approach to morality. This is well-defined. This is challenged effectively by the use of the example of the sale of indulgences. However, the evaluative comment that the 'pillar and bulwark of truth' seems 'coherent' is an assertion rather than analysis. The candidate would need to explain HOW this seems coherent e.g. what is meant by the 'pillar and bulwark of truth' – on what grounds? E.g. could refer to Jesus conferring responsibility to Peter – "what you loose on Earth will be loosed in Heaven" (Matthew 18:18).

Such ethical heteronomy has been challenged by the liberal Catholic Hans Kung, who rejected papal infallibility. Kung argued instead that Christian decisions should be derived from reason through autonomous Christian ethics. Rather than the Church, the principle of agape should be derived from Jesus' statements, as seen in John: 'This is my commandment, that you love one another as I have loved you'. However, Kung's ethics are problematic in that individual reason can lead to different outcomes depending on who is making them. Take, for example, euthanasia – applying agape can either result in people performing euthanasia to ease the suffering of loved ones, or rejecting it because of a desire to spend more time with their family before they die. Individual circumstances and differences of opinion mean that Kung's ideas seem to run the risk of being too antinomian in that it seems to discard the need for moral rules other than to 'love' – and this is a vague way of approaching moral decision-making as working out the most loving thing to do is difficult, changing form situation to situation – a weakness of situation ethics. Furthermore, such thinking may isolate the Church, leaving the individual to act independently, discarding many years of tradition and the teachings of wise scholars who have debated moral issues at length. It seems absurd that the individual would be able to make a more informed choice than the Church scholars. Rather than autonomy, the risk is that the individual is idolised – having more moral authority than the Church or Bible, running a risk of falling into "moral chaos" (Robinson). Arguably, the Church would instead provide structure and order in moral decisions that can make them easier and perhaps fairer to those struggling to make them. A collective decision based on Bible, Church, tradition and reason would be fairer, extending to all and maintaining standards.

An excellent demonstration of knowledge and understanding with a strong focus on the question. Accurate use of technical terms and scholars used to support insightful and critical analysis. Effective linking of Hans Kung to some of the challenges of a situationist approach to moral decision-making.

In contrast, John Calvin challenges Church authority over morality as having been corrupted by human interpretation – he believed that Christian ethics should be derived theonomously through the Bible. Working from the idea that 'all scripture is divinely inspired' (Timothy), Calvin argued that close reading of the scripture allows people to take its commandments at face value rather than trying to twist them to their own ends, as the Catholic Church did initially to attempt to justify the sale of indulgences. However, Calvin's theonomous ethics run the risk of becoming too literalist and focusing on the wording of the Bible rather than its message – Karl Barth referred to this as 'Bibliolatry'. Such a legalistic interpretation of Christian teaching also prevents flexibility on new moral issues. Abortion is never mentioned in the Bible but heteronomous ethics allows the Church to debate on its morality whereas theonomous ethics struggle to find relevant Bible passages. Therefore, the Church does have a place in deciding what is morally right through more coherent readings of the Bible and debate on the meaning of passages, as well as through by helping decide how to deal with new moral issues.

Clear argument and further demonstration of extensive scholar and wisdom and authority' use. Technical – bibliolatry, theonomous etc. Good use of examples, again, to demonstrate argument that the Church does have a role to play in moral decision-making. Though it is not clear yet whether the candidate thinks it should have the only say.

Perhaps the most effective challenge to absolute Church authority comes from Dietrich Bonhoeffer however. Living in Nazi Germany he saw first-hand how the Lutheran Church in the country was taken over by the Nazi party and transformed into the 'Deutsche Evangelische Kirche', a viciously anti-Semitic and pro-Nazi organisation. Bonhoeffer questioned how we could possibly support a state Church that seemed so against Christian teaching and instead argued that 'the man of duty will in the end be forced to give his due': even the Church will be forced through duty to commit evil in the name of the state. Even the Catholic Church was not immune from supporting a regime so self-evident in their evil, as evidenced by the popular pro-Nazi radio broadcasts by Father Charles Coughlin in the United States. The Church is vulnerable to political concerns because it is made up of human beings and is thus fallible. Therefore, I would argue that it would be unwise to rely solely on the Church to determine what is morally right; but neither should it be completely ignored. It would seem sensible to use it as a guide but appreciate that it, too, is fallible.

Superb technicality and effective use of Bonhoeffer to support the candidate's concluding comments. Accurate details build strength to the argument.

While the Church is indeed useful in determining what is ethical as a middle ground between legalistic Calvin and antinomian Kung, I do not believe it can be seen as the sole decider of what is morally good. Its political ties to the world and its capability to become wrong and stuck in its ways means that to best decide what is the most moral course of action, both scripture and reason should be used to provide the best course of action in a given situation –

Christian ethics should be derived heteronomously.

Overall: 36/40 = 90% A*

AO1: L6 [14]

Excellent demonstration of knowledge with thorough, precise use of technical terms and vocabulary in context. Extensive range of academic approaches. Nuanced approach to material with own examples used to illustrate points.

AO2: L6 [22]

Excellent, clear and successful argument with precise focus on question throughout. A sustained and well-developed line of reasoning that is supported by scripture and various scholars and candidate's own interpretations and examples.

To what extent can belief in the existence of purgatory be justified? (26/40 Grade C)

The belief of purgatory is where those who have died in a state of grace, continue to seek forgiveness and receive punishment awaiting Final Judgement. There are three different Christian teachings on heaven, hell and purgatory. One is that heaven, hell and purgatory are actual places. Another is that heaven, hell and purgatory are not places, but spiritual states, that a person experiences as part of their spiritual journey after death. Furthermore, another Christian teaching that heaven, hell and purgatory are symbols of a person's spiritual and moral life on earth and not places or states after death. While ideas about purgatory have remained a part of Catholic doctrine, Protestant beliefs tend to reject it – saying that Jesus' sacrifice allowed for judgement to be immediate, meaning there would be no need for purgatory.

A gentle introductory paragraph introducing the relevant terms. However, the introduction shows a slight danger of the candidate exploring Heaven and Hell too – these would have to be clearly entwined with arguing around the existence of purgatory if this is to be successful. A good link to Catholic and Protestant beliefs is made – it could be a useful argument to tie in evidence of immediate vs final judgement.

Purgatory is a Catholic way of extending the opportunity for repentance beyond this life, even though there is no clear representation of this in the New Testament. However, there is a hint, 1 PETER 3:19 "When made alive, Jesus went to preach to the spirits in the prison". This suggests that in his resurrection, Jesus was able to talk to the spirits of the dead. 'Prison' implies purgatory – a state before being 'free'. Since Christians follow Jesus' example and some believe the Bible to be the infallible word of God this might count as strong justification for the existence of purgatory. However, this might only be the case for those who believe they can continue to seek forgiveness – this would necessitate belief in a Final Judgement, as opposed to the Protestant belief in Immediate Judgement.

Good definition and appropriate link to Catholic belief. Good use of 'wisdom and authority' with the 1 Peter quotation and this is competently explained and linked back to the question. Candidate shows confidence in aligning the views with Catholic or Protestant beliefs and the belief in an ability to continue to seek forgiveness.

Indeed, there is a widespread view that after death those who have died in the state of grace may continue to seek forgiveness for their sins and receive due punishment until final judgement. Arguably, the opportunity for forgiveness is more in line with Christian beliefs in a just and benevolent God ("love thy neighbour" and "God is love"). Thus, purgatory's existence could be justified because it supports Christian teaching towards an omnibenevolent God, as if Hell and Heaven were permanent this implies an unjust God.

Good linking of judgement to God's nature. A response to this that the candidate could engage with is the idea that for God to be just, His punishments would have to be lasting – it depends on what you think justice is.

In later Christian teaching, the idea that there is an intermediate state between death and everlasting life in heaven evolved for two reasons, firstly as a matter of fairness by allowing a person who had not fully prepared themselves for God's final judgement to do so and secondly because of the ambiguity between personal and final judgement. The phrase 'only as through fire', a frequently cited passage in support of purgatory, is the verse from St Paul's letter to the Corinthians. For some, 'only as through fire' is interpreted to be the process of purging or cleansing required when at his personal judgement his works or deeds on Earth were found to be inadequate or 'burned up'. However, many theologians don't find this interpretation at all convincing.

Dante's vision of purgatory is that, for those souls who believe in Christ and have repented before death. They now have the opportunity to purge themselves of all wrongful desires and actions. As they are not unable to sin, the process is entirely positive and is totally unlike hell where punishment perpetuates the initial sin. Dante poetically describes how the soul ascends various 'terraces of the mountain' whose summit or goal is the beatific vision. At the end of the journey the mountain shakes and the soul ascends to heaven. Each of the terraces represents one of the seven deadly sins and is overseen by angels. The soul's driving force is love and increasingly towards the end of the ascent, reason. But the vision of purgatory is not merely a description of what lies in store after death, but an allegory of how life should be lived now. Earth, like the mountain, provides various temptations which the soul has to conquer in its journey to achieve salvation in heaven. Dante's allegory seems to support the idea that purgatory, Heaven and hell could exist only to the extent that they are symbolic representations for the spiritual life lived out on Earth, rather than being actual places.

Although the Catholic Church acknowledges that there is no specific teaching on purgatory in the New Testament, it reasons that ideas such as 'cleansing by the fire' suggest that some sis can be forgiven in this age and some in the age to come. If this is so, then purgatory as a post mortem and interim state is just another stage in the soul's journey to redemption. Purgatory also explains why the church prays for the souls of the departed. This practice predates Christianity. The Catechism refers to the example of Judas Maccabaeus, who prayed that the souls of the dead should be freed from sin. However, it would perhaps be more convincing to argue that Catholics pray for the souls of the dead 'because' purgatory exists; rather than the argument 'purgatory exists 'because' Catholics pray for dead souls'. This is because the conclusion that 'purgatory exists' cannot be deduced naturally from the act of prayer – this is not a causal relationship. Therefore, purgatory exists to the extent that it could be a spiritual state, or even symbolic; but, it existing as a physical realm is not proven convincingly by the observation of prayer.

Although purgatory has a significant place in Catholic theology, its lack of biblical support has meant that many Protestants have rejected it, preferring instead to focus on judgement, heaven and hell. However, many recent Protestant theologians have increasingly seen the value of purgatory, inspired by the arguments of Origen, as it makes sense morally and philosophically to consider the state after death as a continued dynamic journey of soul or self. John Hick argues that the need for an intermediate state makes a great deal of logical sense as the 'gap between the individuals imperfection at the end of time. Hick argues that it makes more sense to think of the afterlife as a continuation of the 'person-making process' started on Earth where there are many intermediate states which people pass through on their journey to being finally united with God.

Good referencing to Hick. Candidate needs to make stronger links with their line of argument. They seem to be saying purgatory exists but they are not making clear in what sense it exists…

Overall:26/40 65% C

AO1:L5 [11]

Bottom band 5 because the candidate does have a very good selection of material, accurate and detailed knowledge and a good range of academic approaches.

However, at times, the answer loses focus on the question and focuses on just exploring different ideas about purgatory, rather than how convincing this is.

AO2:L4 [15]

Generally successful analysis, at times insightful, well-stated and developed. However, the line of argument does not seem consistent or clear in places and so cannot reach the band 5 of 'coherent development'.

"The doctrine of Election is incompatible with belief in a just God". Discuss (39/40 A*)

Ideas about election present the view that God chooses which people will enter heaven, even before they are created. The implication of this is that God's perfect knowledge of the eternal destiny of each human would mean the role of human choice in determining their spiritual state through good acts, as taught in the Parable of the Sheep and the Goats, would seem pointless. If God has 'elected' only some who will be saved or damned before they have a chance to live (limited election), then there seems little point in trying to 'be good'. This seems to conflict with the idea of a just God as arguably, justice can only be served if the person can be held responsible for their actions. On the other hand, someone might argue that God is just and elects everyone for salvation (unlimited election); but only some respond. In this way, God is just. While unlimited election seems more compatible with belief in a just God than limited election, a universalist position (holding no-one elect) seems most compatible with God's justice.

Excellent introduction introducing the scope of the question, involving both limited and unlimited election and how these relate to God's justice. Candidate's argument is signposted.

Some might argue that the doctrine of Election is incompatible with belief in a just God because it is inherently exclusive. *Nice opening sentence linking directly with the question.* St Augustine developed a belief in limited election. Augustine disagreed with the Pelagianism of his time which taught that people were born tabular rasa and could earn their place in Heaven. Augustine taught that people were born with a post-Lapsarian Original Sin and were therefore sinful from creation. Augustine taught that salvation was not something everyone 'had a right to' in their natural state, as in their natural state, they were sinful. Furthermore, Augustine taught that humans could not reach God's standards through their own efforts, but only through God's grace. Augustine moved from believing God has perfect foreknowledge of people's destiny (and their free choices within this); to believing that God did not only know who would be saved, but He chose who would receive his saving grace and be freed from Original Sin.

Excellent knowledge and understanding of Augustine. Good technicality. Needs linking to argument.

Scripture that supports Augustine's view is Romans – "those he predestined, he also called"; and Ephesians – "in him we were also chosen, having been predestined according to the plan of him". *Good linking with sources of wisdom and authority.* On the one hand, Augustine's limited election could be compatible with belief in a just God as it shows the extension of God's grace. No human deserves eternal life with God and so the extension of this grace and offering of redemption through Jesus Christ – even if only to a few – is evidence of God's benevolence and mercy and therefore compatible with a just God.

The beginnings of a holistic argument, engaging strongly with understanding of Augustine.

However, while this extension of grace might be benevolent, it does not support an 'omni'-benevolent God as suggested by John – "God is love". Augustine's teaching also seems uncompromising and leaves little to no room for human free will. If Jesus is "the way, the truth and the life" – surely humans should be able to choose this path. John Calvin developed Augustine's teaching on election and taught that God was absolute sovereign and nothing could happen outside of God's knowledge or control – including human choice. In this way, God must have pre-ordained those for salvation. However; the idea of God having perfect knowledge of things does not mean he controls these. Indeed, the belief that God controls everything seems incompatible with a just God. It seems more coherent to postulate a God who has Divine Providence (Boethius) of all things 'simultaneously present' to Him (perfect knowledge of human free choice); than for God to control these things and be unable to reward and punish justly. Indeed, if, as Calvin argues, God is controller and 'knower', then humans do not have freedom to do differently to that which God knows and as a result, could not be 'judged' fairly since they were not free to do that for which they are being judged.

The candidate implies, through excellent engagement with Calvin and Boethius, that Calvinist election is not fully compatible with a just God. This argument needs to be made more explicit, however.

A more coherent approach to election that is more compatible with belief in a just God, is that of unlimited election. *Evaluative language – 'more coherent'. Good explanation of Barth follows.* Karl Barth developed this in Church Dogmatics – presenting the idea that Jesus Christ bought salvation for the whole world. Barth wrote about election in terms of choice – that God chose to send Jesus – the elected man, into the world. Barth tried to combine the idea that people are only saved if God chooses and not through their own efforts; with the idea that a loving and just God would not choose only a few for salvation. Barth wrote that Jesus is "both the electing God and elected man in One". The election of individuals is wrapped up with the election of Jesus as their representative, and Jesus is elected so that everyone might have the possibility of eternal life.

Barth's view of unlimited election seems more compatible with Christian belief in a just God as God elected Jesus to enable the possibility of salvation timelessly for all. This is supported by 1 John – "he [Jesus] is the atoning sacrifice for our sins, and not only for ours but also for the sins of the whole world". This passage seems to be more optimistic than Augustine and Calvin's limited election as the salvation is extended to all. Furthermore, 1 Timothy supports Barth to the extent that it focusses on the key role of the elected Jesus in being the "one mediator between God and mankind". Jesus is "the way, the truth and the life" (John) and God intended to "save the world through him" (John 3). 1 Timothy also pays heed to God's benevolence, claiming God "wants all people to be saved and to come to a knowledge of the truth". To an extent, Barth's theology overcomes the problem posed by the limitation Augustine's and Calvin's placed on human freedom in salvation. Barth's views allow everyone the possibility of eternal life if they turn to Christ. In this sense, the 'universal' aspect seems more compatible with belief in a just God.

Strong links are being made to the signposted argument in the introduction that a universalist election approach might be more compatible with a just God. Good use of sources of wisdom and authority. Hick's universalism is brought in shortly.

However, one could argue that Barth's theology is not completely 'unlimited' since due to cultural differences, there will always be some who will never encounter the Gospel and who might grow up in a variety of religious traditions. Despite never encountering the Gospels, people seem capable of doing good acts. It would seem unjust *Candidate's own opinion coming through as part of a sustained argument* for these people to be denied salvation based on their cultural circumstance. John Hick recognised this spending time in multicultural Birmingham and witnessing the good committed by a variety of faiths.

Hick postulated that God would save all people, whatever their beliefs. This is a universalist position and proposes that the afterlife offers the opportunity for everyone to reach God and to develop a choice for God. Hick viewed each religion as a different expression of the universal human desire for God. There is no right or wrong religion, only different traditions of doctrine and practice stemming from cultural differences. Hick's doctrine means that everyone is saved and no one is elected above anyone else. Support for Hick can be found in the Parable of the Sheep and Goats (Matthew 25). *Uses sources of wisdom and authority to develop Hick.* The analogy of those clothing the naked, feeding the hungry etc and Jesus' teaching that "whatever you did for one of the least of these brothers and sisters of mine, you did for me"; focuses on the actions of people leading to their salvation or condemnation. This is in stark contrast to Augustine's teaching that humans cannot achieve salvation through their own deeds. *Nice comparison and links back to compatibility of Election* The teaching also seems more compatible with a just God than the doctrine of election as God would seem able to serve justice if humans were choosing good or bad acts, rather than behaving according to his plan. The parable also teaches that these good/ bad actions reflect human treatment of God/ Jesus. This leaves open the possibility that those who do good deeds outside of Christianity could also be seen to be reflecting Jesus' teaching even if the agent himself is not aware of Jesus' teachings. This supports Hick's universalist approach to salvation and is compatible with belief in a just God.

Strong links using the words of the question statement make the argument coherent.

Overall, neither the limited (Augustine, Calvin) nor the unlimited (Barth) doctrine of election are fully compatible with belief in a just God. This is mainly because of the limitations placed on human free will and the resulting challenge to God rewarding and punishing justly. A universalist approach to salvation allows for humans to freely choose to do good and be rewarded for this; while not excluding those born outside of encountering the Gospels. It seems most compatible with an omnibenevolent and just God.

Overall: 39/40 98% = Grade A *

AO1: Level 6 [16]

Thorough knowledge and understanding of Augustine, Calvin, Bath and Hick shown. Each scholar is linked with sources of wisdom and authority and is used to engage with the philosophical problems raised by belief in a just God. Links are made to benevolence and the problem of free will.

AO2: Level 6 [23]

Critical and insightful analysis throughout and an extensive range of scholarly views skilfully assessed to reach an insightful conclusion.

To what extent was Jesus just a teacher of morality? (36/40 Grade A)

Jesus' moral teaching comes as part of his being a teacher of wisdom in developing Jewish ethics. However, he can also be seen as a liberator of the poor and marginalised in his challenging of political and religious authorities, as well as the Son of God brought into the earth to bring salvation and carry out God's will on Earth. Arguably, however, these three roles are interlinked, with his authority as a liberator and teacher of wisdom stemming from being the Messiah.

Strong, confident introduction providing context for the question and also signposting the candidate's thoughts. Candidate shows awareness of the scope of the question.

Firstly, the perception of Jesus as a teacher of wisdom and morality is largely seen through his use of parables and the Sermon on the Mount influencing Jewish ethics. The Sermon on the Mount is considered to be the focal point of Jesus' moral teachings. Within this Sermon he taught the need for reconciliation rather than retribution, which can be seen in his Parable of the Lost Son. In this parable the younger son takes his inheritance and spends it all on a frivolous and selfish lifestyle, on returning to his father, after realising his mistakes, his father forgives him. Whilst it easy to condemn the older brother for his resentment toward his brother, and seeming inability to forgive him, it is through him that Jesus conveys that despite the hardship of true forgiveness we should strive for it, as only then can we be set free mentally to start a fresh and lead a life of morality. *Good, an insightful commentary on the moral teaching here.* This enforces Jesus' teachings on the Mount, where he teaches that the new covenant is about developing appropriate virtues of inner law, love and righteousness and not merely following the rules and laws laid out by the Old testament, but the ten commandments are still the basis for his teachings.

Good, technical language.

However, some would argue that what Jesus' teaching stresses too much the future ideal state of the Kingdom of God, as did the prophets in the Old testament; whereas in this imperfect world evil and suffering are considered 'necessary' as part of our growth, learning right from wrong (part of our 'soul-making' if we use Irenaeus' and Hick's theodicies). This implies Jesus might have been more than a teacher of morality when he is preaching God's Kingdom. There is also the idea, in the Sermon on the Mount, that Jesus could be seen as an 'enforcer' of morality rather than a teacher, since the moral law could be seen as innate in us – St Paul taught that "the law of God is written on the hearts of all" – perhaps Jesus is exposing this rather than teaching this.

Some insightful, nuanced evaluation here considering different ideas about Jesus as teacher or 'enforcer' or morality. Candidate is engaging well with the sources of wisdom and authority chosen.

Although Jesus might seem much more than a teacher of morality to a Christian who would seem him also as Son of God; the notion of Jesus just as a teacher of morality appeals to a multi-faith society, where Jesus' teachings are based around the central idea of reconciliation and love of ones enemies. However, arguably both these ideas are discernible by reason and are evident in religious and non-religious society. This could lead us to question whether Jesus' teachings are no more than enforcing of what is innate human moral knowledge, leading us to think that Jesus was just an a-enforcer of morality rather than a teacher. But philosophers such as Wittgenstein would refute this claiming that Jesus as a teacher of morality affirmed authentic living in speaking out against hypocrisy as well as his commitment to the truth. For Wittgenstein Jesus was not abstract an idea but rather the 'living word', embodying the external moral and inner spiritual life, which goes against this notion that Jesus was just a teacher of morality but rather he gains authority on such issues of morality through his connection to the spiritual as the Son of God.

Really strong, insightful links being made here. The candidate is widening the scope of the question and is engaging with the implications for both the religious and non-religious community. The candidate has followed through from the introduction, to link Jesus as moral teacher, to his being the 'son of God', and this is cleverly been informed by Wittgenstein.

The phrase 'Son of God' was often used to refer to the anointed one, whose responsibility was in giving hope that Israel would be freed politically, morally and spiritually. The Hebrew for 'anointed one' was Messiah, or the Greek word Christos, meaning that Son of God. Christ is an equivalent. In this sense we can create a link between the Jesus of morality and Jesus as the Son of God, as the anointed one to save the morality of the Israelites.

A fair attempt at pulling together the language of Messiah and Christ and linking this with Jesus as moral 'saviour'. Could perhaps be supported by Scripture references – one Old, one New, to link the Jewish ideas of Messiah and Jesus' fulfilment of this (in Christians' eyes).

A large part of the interpretation of Jesus as the Son of God is seen through the miracles he performed over his life time, the most notable one being of his resurrection and ascension into heaven. Jesus' death on the cross can be seen as a last earthly teaching in sacrificing himself for the sins of others. He sets an example, not of giving up your life for others but rather implying that the biggest reward is in sacrifice. Even for those who discount some of the miracles stories, Jesus' resurrection is still considered to be the significant moment in revealing his divinity as the Son of God. Pannenberg dismisses the miracles, rather choosing to argue that Jesus' resurrection is the sole moment than 'visibly and unambiguously' reveals him as God in that it is uniquely a sign of

God's completion and perfection at the end of time. Despite his ascension to heaven Jesus' teachings still live on, being looked toward as confirmation of authentic living, despite many of the miracles being reinterpreted to be symbolic rather than literal.

How can the candidate link this back to the question? What implication does Jesus' resurrection and Pannenberg have for Jesus as teacher of morality? Is it that his moral teachings liv eon but his Divinity enables this?

Another of his miracles that gave hope of salvation is the healing of a blind man's sight (John 9:41), but it is miracles such as this that those of both religious and non-religious belief have been sceptical of, choosing rather to understand them as parables, with an underlying meaning. The understanding of this parable is not so much on how he receives his sight but the bringing of his sight to see God and understanding Jesus as the saviour and the inability of those with the sight to truly see and be at one with their faith. Therefore, from this we could understand Jesus to be no more than a teacher of wisdom and morality, who's miracles should be interpreted similar to his parables, in containing an underlying meaning.

Good link back to the question. Good use of wisdom and authority to maintain a line of argument that appeared lost in the previous paragraph.

However, Jesus' teachings of the Kingdom of God ~~were~~ might not just be spiritual preparation for the coming age but a call to alter the current structures of society. For example, Jesus can be seen as a liberator of the marginalized. S. G. F. Brandon views the historical Jesus as a politically driven freedom fighter believing later accounts of him in the Gospels re-wrote passages to convey him rather as a pacifist. This notion of Jesus as a liberator is particularly attractive in areas where there has been considerable class antagonism and exploitation. Liberation theologians found inspiration in this presentation of Jesus believing him to have been presented as politically neutral for too long, preaching spiritual values without desiring to alter unjust economic social structures. However, this is an idea that can be disputed in looking at passages such as Luke where Jesus helped transform the tax collector. Gutiérrez argues that whilst we can view Jesus as a Zealot he was much more than that. It is through the example set by Jesus in Luke chapter 19 that we can see that his authority and success as a liberator stems from his role as teacher of wisdom and morality. *Again, nice link back to line of argument – sustained, insightful, technical and informed by wisdom and authority.*

Overall, scholars find the depiction of Jesus as a liberator to be powerful as it creates a model by which we can use to challenge an unjust world, whilst others find Jesus' authority was not political but rather of a spiritual nature. However, within parables such as the Good Samaritan Jesus conveys that it is not only our political duty to aid the marginalised but also our moral and spiritual duty, which indicates that His authority is found in the intertwined nature of Jesus as a liberator and Jesus the teacher of morality.

Overall: 36/40 90% A*

AO1: L6 [15]

Fully comprehending the demands of the question. Excellent selection of material that is used skillfully to address the areas of the question the candidate identified in the introduction. A 'nuanced' approach tying together the different aspects of Jesus studied.

AO2: L6 [21]Views skilfully stated, coherently developed. In places, confident and critical analysis with lots of evidence of candidate's own voice coming through.

"Christian values are more than just basic human values: they have something distinctive to offer." Discuss (36/40 Grade A*)

Christian values have often been identified as compassion, forgiveness, justice, and peace. However, these can also be described as essential human values, furthering society without having to turn to belief in an afterlife of a saviour Lord. However, the claim that Christian values are 'distinctive' seems to separate the spiritual from the human and this would conflict with the message of the incarnation – God bringing together the human and divine.

This introduction identifies some Christian values that will form part of their argument and it introduces the implication of the spiritual vs human debate.

Firstly, the Gospels set the example of Christian values of compassion, forgiveness, justice and peace. For example, the parable of the Prodigal son and his forgiving father show forgiveness and compassion; Jesus' many healing miracles – of the blind man, the paralysed man, taking spirits out of a boy etc also show Jesus' compassion and the example is set for us to follow. Jesus teaches us to consider the plank of wood in our own eye before addressing the splinter in another's – showing us that justice involves looking inwardly before addressing others. Furthermore, when Jesus is asked about who should throw the first stone at an adulterous woman, he says 'let he who has not sinned throw the first stone' and all walk away. These teachings show that justice is not always 'passing judgement' – it also shows we are responsible for our own moral development too.

Here, the candidate shows the source of these Christian values, using the Bible and Jesus' own example as a source of wisdom and authority.

However, there does not seem to be anything distinctive about these values – perhaps Jesus was interpreting a concern for humanity that was challenging society of the day, but in no different a way to the ways in which the Suffragettes went on to challenge attitudes to the roles of women, and the way in which society raises concerns for the rights of the LGBTQ community today. Perhaps Christian 'values' represent values arising out of society. For example, compassion and love is reassuring for people and creates a positive experience of life. Forgiveness is an important part of overcoming failures within the self and within relationships. Justice enables a fair approach to wrong-doing and peace furthers society, in contrast to the destructive forces of war. Enhancing society based on these values keeps society from falling into chaos. Since we can articulate such a moral code without reference to belief in God or an afterlife, then we could say that 'Christian values' are no more than basic human values and are far from distinctive.

Now, the candidate justifies the same values as arising out of society and makes a case for the values not being distinctive, showing good engagement with the question.

Indeed, Richard Dawkins teaches that life has meaning without reference to religion – "there is something infantile in the presumption that somebody else...has a responsibility to give your life meaning." In his argument that religion is something for children to escape from and is harmful, Dawkins draws attention to the abuse of children among Church ministers, the Hell House example in Colorado and the 19th century kidnapping of Jewish children who were then baptised and raised Catholic. While these examples are extreme, they seem to contradict the values of peace, forgiveness and justice that were earlier identified as 'Christian'. It seems here, that the only 'distinctive' feature of these so-called Christian values, is that they seem distorted in practice and conflicts with general values of love. Society seems to abhor some of the religious ideas of justice – for example, the 'cutting off of offending hands' in Matthew 9 and the eternal damnation in hell for homosexuality or sexual immorality (1 Corinthians 6).

Dawkins is brought in as a scholarly view and is used to claim that the Christian values seem contradicted by Christian action and teaching in the Bible. Interestingly, they make the point that the values might be 'distinctive' but for the wrong reasons.

However, one could argue that this would be missing the point. Jesus' central message was to 'love your neighbour as yourself' and to 'love God'. Jesus taught to put yourself last – that the "first will be last and the last, first", that we should be a servant to our brethren. The teachings of Paul in Corinthians do not match with this message of love for outcasts. The Christian values of self-sacrificial unconditional love arguably cannot be explained using the rationality of love, peace and justice above. For example, nuns travelling to Ebola-stricken areas to administer aid, or a mother giving her life for a son does not seem to be explained purely in terms of the functioning of society. Similarly, the Christian teachings of loving your enemy and 'turning the other cheek', extending love to a foreigner – all seem to go against what is easier and safer to do. This implies that such values arise form a commitment to something greater and 'outside of' oneself – something distinctive. Such values seem based on an appreciation of the intrinsic worth of all humans as made imago dei and in this way, can be seen as distinctive.

A strong alternative argument bringing balance to the essay and engaging with what it means to be 'distinctive', bringing in values other than those in the introduction.

Notwithstanding, even the values from society seem to be based on a shared understanding of the intrinsic worth of humans. We have a Universal Declaration of Human Rights – for all, despite individual (robbery, murder) and collective (pollution) wrong-doing. This suggests that society appreciates humans as having some form of intrinsic worth – which is why even inmates get basic human rights such as food, water, shelter and hygiene and health facilities.

Overall, it seems most convincing to suggest that spiritual and human values cannot be separate. It is not a case that Christian values are 'no more' than basic human values; but rather, human values are inherently of a spiritual nature too. *Excellent engagement with the demands of the question.* This can be supported by some Christian teaching. The belief in Christianity that God took on human form and became man and lived among us, lends itself to the idea that in encountering other humans, we are also encountering God. God's incarnation brings humans into new fellowship with Him – made final in Christ's death and resurrection. God represents both the divine and the human and in this way, human values cannot be made separate to Christian values. In a similar way, Christian values cannot be seen as distinctive to human values.

Overall: 36/40 = 90% Grade A*

AO1: Level 6 [14]   The candidate uses an excellent range of Biblical texts as a source of authority and engages strongly with the question of 'values' – even contrasting these with Christian action as referenced by Dawkins. The question is answered precisely throughout through a balanced discussion of the different views concerning values and whether they are 'human' or 'spiritual'. Perhaps some Church teaching and other secular challenges could be brought in as scholar references.

AO2: Level 6 [22] The candidate shows skilfully developed argument and appropriate selection of scholarly views. Insightful conclusion equating the human with the spiritual.

Assess the view that Bonhoeffer's teaching on ethics still has relevance today. (29/40 Grade B)

Bonhoeffer's main teachings on ethics include 'duty to God and to the state', and the 'cost' of discipleship. For these teachings to still be relevant today, they would need to address global politics, be compatible with plural moral societies and multi-faith societies. Bonhoeffer's teaching on 'costly grace' seems most relevant in relation to questioning oppression and siding with the marginalised. However, perhaps theology is not best placed to deal with matters arising in a secular world.

This introduction shows good links to the specification, knowledge of Bonhoeffer's main teachings and the issues today that might be relevant. The candidate's argument is also signposted.

Firstly, Bonhoeffer generally agreed with the Lutheran teaching on obedience as state ruling was seen to bring order to the sinful human natural tendency towards disorder. However, he recognised that sometimes, the state gains too much power and justice can be set below policies and the state can try to justify any action by claiming it is 'justice itself'. By this, Bonhoeffer would say that the state fails to acknowledge its obedience to the will of God. Bonhoeffer argued that the state can never represent the will of God and so can never have ultimate power. The role of the Church is to keep the state in check – and not be a part of it. *Good introduction to Bonhoeffer's views on obedience to the state. A short quotation would be handy as a source.*

Some might say that in the context of global politics and plural societies, the role of the Church is much more limited. Christian ethics were formed outside of secular society and should have no relevance to our more secular society today. Jesus taught "give to Caesar what is Caesar's and to God what is God's"; and Romans taught "let everyone be subject to the governing authorities, for there is no authority except that which God has established." These Biblical teachings imply that even if the Bible was a source of inspiration for a religious relationship with the state, obedience would still be an important part of this. Perhaps this is why many Christians would be content serving their country in war, despite the teaching 'do not kill'. *Candidate seems to be suggesting that Bonhoeffer's teachings are relevant since obedience to the state was directed in the Bible and state obedience is still shown today. However, this link is not made explicit.*

However, Bonhoeffer would say we are asking the 'wrong question' if we are asking ourselves simply whether it is morally good to obey the state. *Good – showing more comprehensive understanding of Bonhoeffer.* Rather, we should ask whether obeying the state is God's will. "The nature of this will of God can only be clear in the moment of action" and as an act of faith, not personal ambition. Bonhoeffer was not a moral relativist (as misinterpreted by Fletcher). He did not think acting 'out of love' was sufficient as this reduces God to a human idea. Regarding disobeying the state, the killing of Hitler would only be justified by "bold action as the free response to faith". However, knowing God's will in the moment of action must be difficult to discern – unless we accept that God inspires us to act in faith and any thought to consequences would always be inaccurate. Some might say that this teaching is not just irrelevant but extremely impractical in the complexities of living in a multi-faith and cultural society today – it would not be enough to claim that "I act in faith" when the matters concern education, housing, and health. We have many state leaders and if each decided to act in faith – whom can we trust? Bonhoeffer offered consolation by saying God promises to forgive the "man who becomes a sinner in the process" of obeying God's will. However, this gives little consolation for those acting and living in the present.

Bonhoeffer's teachings on ethics also include his teachings on the 'cost' of discipleship. Rather than accepting that Christian ethics are outside of our secular world, Bonhoeffer asserted that Christianity is grounded in the everyday world – it is not an 'otherworldly institution' and in this way, is relevant today. This 'in-worldliness' is seen is God's incarnation as Jesus. We should focus less on God's nature and more on who Christ is for us today. This involves both a hearing of, and action according to, God's will – both the Pharisees and Martha in Luke failed to do both. Authentic Christian living must be based on Christ, scripture, and faith. Since religion is a human invention-just like politics, the Church must be kept separate from the state if it is to avoid being politically manipulated. By taking on the world, a Christian disciple endangers himself. God's grace cannot be won over by rituals – this would be 'cheap grace'. Rather, God's grace is 'costly' – "because it cost man his life, and it is grace because it gives man the only true life." The greatest cost is seen in God's loss of his Son.

Bonhoeffer's teaching on costliness seems to have significant relevance today. Bonhoeffer's teachings came at a time when he realised he might have to die standing against evil ('Letters from Prison'). Bonhoeffer called for solidarity with the Jews and those afflicted by Nazism. Bonhoeffer's teaching that Jesus was 'the man for others' called for the Church to fight the evil of discrimination. Bonhoeffer called for a full engagement in resistance against injustice – "not just to bandage the victims under the wheel, but to put a spoke in the wheel itself." This relevance in the face of global politics today gives place to Christianity as a spiritual conscience in the state's involvement in politics – e.g. the role of the Bishops in the House of Lords as voices spiritual. *Good to bring back to practicality of state vs religion today.* Furthermore, Stanley Hauerwas *good to have a scholar link* would claim that Bonhoeffer's concern for truth is a much needed challenge to the pragmatic democracy of the West – tolerance should not get in the way of truth. This is particularly relevant in a plural moral society as in modern times, the focus on tolerance seems to involve being non-judgemental of various moral viewpoints. Being non-judgemental, however, is different from being 'just' and this is where Bonhoeffer is more helpful.

However, overall, despite Bonhoeffer working to free the oppressed, he still maintained that the Jews should convert to Christianity eventually. Despite Bonhoeffer's important emphasis that the state should give equal rights and protection to all citizens, his theology of Christianity as a spiritual conscience might be incompatible with the multi-faith West. Bonhoeffer's ethics targeted the singular threat of Nazism and today, there is a greater diversity of significant threats with extremism. It seems that Bonhoeffer's greatest relevance in this regard, would be his focus on tolerance not replacing truth as just being 'tolerant' can lead to indifference and this is where tyranny arises. The difficulty remains, however, in recognising this truth.

Overall: 29/40 73% Grade B

AO1: Level 5 [12]

Very good knowledge and understanding of Bonhoeffer's views and generally, a very good focus on the question set. More could be done in terms of linking it to issues today – in what way can Bonhoeffer's ethics specifically engage with issues arising from plural moral and faith societies? Or can it not do this? This would raise the answer to level 6.

AO2: Level 5 [17]

The conclusion brings this answer into level 5, rather than 4 as it shows the incompatibility of Bonhoeffer's teachings but a strength of Bonhoeffer's focus on truth. It suggests the problem of recognising this truth remains a limitation and so the answer to the question of relevance is not a simple one. The candidate engages with some strengths and weaknesses but the argument is not always clear.

'Bonhoeffer's most important teaching is on leadership'. Discuss. (31/40 Grade B)

Bonhoeffer's main teachings can be divided up into duty to God and state; discipleship and the Church as a community. Arguably, leadership threads through each of these topics and so cannot clearly be separated as the 'most important'- though it makes more of an impact and therefore, is more important in his teaching on duty to God and state, compared to his teachings on discipleship. However, we must not always follow his teaching on leadership, where civil obedience is shown, such as Bonhoeffer's resistance against Nazism.

An interesting introduction that addresses the question and proposes a line of argument that suggests 'leadership' imbues the scope of Bonhoeffer's teachings, rather than being a branch of teaching to be judged independently. The final sentence leads to a little confusion and one would hope that this would be addressed in the body of the essay.

Bonhoeffer's teaching on duty to God and duty to state is that Christians have a responsibility to the state, which they must work together on to ensure the state acts in accordance to God's will. The state often fails to acknowledge its obedience to the will of God. *Example needed.* In traditional Christian teaching we must obey the state and God, because Luther taught that there are two kingdoms ordained by God, the spiritual governed by the Church and the political governed by the state. For example, in Matthew 22:21 Jesus answered a question from the Pharisees and Herodians on taxes 'Give to Caesar what is Caesar's, and to God what is God's'. This implies that individuals have an obligation to God and to the state – the latter of which was also thought to be ordained by God. However, the question that arises is how are we supposed to know what God's will is and whether the state is obeying it?   Bonhoeffer's

203

reply in No Rusty Swords is that we need to act with faith which will 'only be clear in the moment of action'. With regard to leadership, Bonhoffer's teaching implies that both the Divine and the state lead are of importance. However, 'leadership' is not as clear as following a set example. Rather, Bonhoeffer's call to act in faith that will "be clear in the moment of action" is suggestive of a type of leadership that is conscience-driven, something innate that represents a discernment of the right course of action. This teaching on leadership is striking as it is different to the legalistic approach to following Divine and State law.

Good example of scripture, coherently developed and justified with accurate reference to scholars. While the 'importance' of the teaching is not clear, the candidate does build an analysis on the teaching in order to mark it as 'distinct'.

Arguably, though, humans can make mistakes on impulse and often do not think through decisions carefully. We need to work out what God's will is through the use of the Bible as a guideline and using our reason as Kant would say edging us towards the summon bonum and allowing us to live autonomously. It is unreasonable to suggest that we will know what God's will is in 'the moment of action', we do not always suddenly work things out when faced with a question, situation or problem to solve. Leadership here is being taught by that we must follow God's will and the state's laws. We need to follow the state's laws to an extent, because otherwise, we would be in a state of chaos and society would never function altogether, we need certain laws and rules such as murder is wrong and these need to be punishable. Otherwise, many people would have no morals and know what is right from wrong, because there would be no justice. This suggests that while Bonhoeffer's teaching on leadership with regard to following the state and God is distinctive; its importance would depend on its impact and clarity. It seems that it is not enough to simply 'know in the moment of action'.

A nice link to Kant and the use of Bible and reason to develop our understanding.

However, this could be developed to make the argument that perhaps Bonhoeffer's teaching on leadership is important but not clear. Candidate does develop the point that it is not enough to rely on knowing 'in the moment of action'. A line of argument is being developed.

However, although leadership is a part of Bonhoeffer's teaching on duty to God and duty to state, it is not the most important part of it, but civil disobedience is. *A confident and coherent statement of evaluation.* Christians have a duty to disobey if the state is acting immoral 'making people face unreasonable situations', because that is not in accordance with God's will. For example, Bonhoeffer, became part of the resistance of Nazism, such as delivering a radio broadcast in 1933 against Hitler's regime, joining the confessing Church and constructing a community at Finkenwalde training clergy for the Confessing Church. *Accurate knowledge.* It was triggered by the German Christian movement and the 'Aryan Paragraph'. Martin Niemoeller as well as Bonhoeffer disagreed with the change and brought others who disagreed as well together, forming the Confessing Church. *Explain what this did in order to show 'highly detailed knowledge'.* Therefore, we should not always follow a regime, idea or law even if it is widely held as right. Bertrand Russel, for example would support, because leaders do not always instruct commands and rules morally and acceptable for society. What is more important than Bonhoeffer's teaching on leadership is to decide for yourself what is the right thing to do not necessarily in accordance to God's will but assessing what is morally right in today's world and not supporting a view just because it is widely held. This is more important, because otherwise we start to lose our autonomy in obeying unjustifiable situations and   makes people with more authority have more importance as a human being. In Proverbs 22:2 'Rich and poor have this in common: The LORD is the Maker of them all', we are all made equally by God and therefore, leadership is not the most important teaching, because obeying to a leader is not always the morally good decision when they often do not act in solidarity and put themselves before others instead.

Relevant material and good to see Russell and Proverbs references. A nuanced approach to material selected and a clear argument that leadership is not the most important teaching; but instead, civil disobedience – a recognition of improper/ immoral leadership is more important. One could argue, however, that this was Bonhoeffer's point, and it still relates to leadership.

Furthermore, another one of Bonhoeffer's teachings is discipleship, of following the life, teaching and example of Jesus. We should be looking at 'who is Christ for us today?', rather than investigating God's divinity. Karl Barth taught Bonhoeffer that we do not know God but that he chooses to reveal Himself to us, which is a special act shown in the person and life of Jesus Christ. However, Bonhoeffer did not think Barth went far enough. If we believe that only God can act in our world then we become just passive recipients of his revelation, we must 'do' as well as 'hear' the law. For example, in Luke 10:38-42 'Martha was distracted by all the preparations', we do not always listen to what is important but get distracted by other things. We have conscience which experiences disunity in self, God and others and prompts action. Ethics is action- liberating. For example, in America Bonhoeffer decided to go back to Germany and engage in the 'terrible alternative', to experience the terrors of the Nazi regime with his people, because he believed that it was his duty. For Bonhoeffer, it was important for us to be separate from the state, however, it can come at a cost, of taking on an unjust society. God's grace has to be 'costly', because it costs man's life, the sacrifice of Jesus. 'Cheap grace' is disregarded, God's grace cannot be bought or just by following Christian rituals, it requires to sacrifice a lot more than that. Bonhoeffer's time in prison supports 'Costly grace' and that he would ultimately have to sacrifice his life. He adopted Barth's word of 'krisis'. Because there is crisis in the world (Christian paradox), such as sin, therefore, it means that God reveals 'crisis'. Leadership is taught here to be a disciple and follow the life of Jesus Christ, by sacrificing your own life and following 'costly grace'. The importance of this teaching is that it simultaneously talks of leadership within community through costly discipleship, and the leadership one develops through autonomously opting to take on the unjust society and choosing orthopraxis over orthodoxy.

Again, good bringing in of scripture as a source of wisdom and authority to support analysis. Knowledge of 'costly grace' used to argue for a specific, nuanced perspective eon the leadership aspect of Bonhoeffer's teaching. The candidate makes strong links back to the question at the end of the paragraph – as has been done in previous paragraphs this contributes to a coherently developed argument.

However, Bonhoeffer places too much on emphasis on suffering, it is unreasonable to suggest that you must follow Jesus' life to the extent that you must sacrifice your life. This would be a contradiction against the first formulation of Kant's categorical imperative – we could not universally be prepared to sacrifice our lives believing it to be in the name of God, since the possibility of a depletion of humanity would exist. It would also not be a positive thing for an ordered society and would therefore, go against one of Aquinas' primary precepts. If you live a Christian life of love and peace then it is unnecessary. Additionally, Bonhoeffer forgets the significance of the resurrection, Jesus' passion represents triumph over death and sin not just suffering. Therefore, leadership in this teaching of discipleship is not the most important. Rather leadership in Bonhoeffer's teaching of duty to God and duty to state is much more important, because it recognizes the importance of constructing an ordered society.

An interesting link with Kant and Thomas Aquinas, developing a breadth of response. The concluding evaluative comments on leadership being more important in 'duty to God' than in 'costly grace' is insightful and would ideally be developed to show why the 'construction of an ordered society' is more important than the notion of sacrifice.

Bonhoeffer's teaching on leadership is very important and gives a lot of impact because there is an element of it in all his teachings and helps to create an ordered society to an extent. However, it is not the most important, we should not always follow leadership rigidly, otherwise we can start to lose our autonomy and we can act immorally in some situations. We need to take inspiration and honour Jesus' life, not copy it.

Overall: 31/40 78% Grade B

AO1: L5 [13]

Very good demonstration of knowledge and a focus on the question throughout. Accurate and appropriate use of technical terms – including more innovative uses of Natural Moral Law and Kantian Ethics to develop the argument.

To reach level 6, the candidate would need to develop the relevance of the community at Finkenwalde and the Church as community as mentioned in the introduction.

AO2: L5 [18]

Answers the question set competently with some clearly stated views that are coherently developed. The look at leadership in duty and discipleship was nuanced and a good range of sources of wisdom and authority were used.

To reach level 6, candidate could explain what t would mean for 'leadership' to be important in Bonhoeffer's teaching – is it that it has an impact or that it is clear? Candidate makes an interesting point about acting autonomously rather than necessarily following the leader – could this autonomy, however, be a form of self-leadership?

"A theologically pluralist approach significantly undermines the central doctrines of Christianity." Discuss (32/40 Grade A)

A 'theologically pluralist' approach is one which holds the view that there are several means of salvation through different religious traditions. This is a view supported by Hick but challenged by exclusivist beliefs that hold faith in Christ to be 'the way' and not 'a way' to salvation; and inclusivist beliefs that say that Christianity sets the standard for salvation. Some of the central doctrines of Christianity include the Virgin Birth, incarnation, and the doctrine of salvation through Christ's death and resurrection. Theological pluralism does seem to significantly undermine the Christian doctrines of salvation through Christ and punishment for those who do not accept Christ. However, it is difficult to agree on which doctrines are central to Christianity.

A strong opening paragraph. It defines the 'theological pluralist' approach and raises the issues of it being challenged by inclusivism and exclusivism. It also signposts the direction of the essay by suggesting that some doctrines are challenged, but there might be more important ones that remain unchallenged.

Firstly, one proponent of theological pluralism is John Hick. Hick proposed a 'Copernican revolution' in our approach to theology, saying we should put God central, not doctrine. Kant taught that there is a difference between the noumenal world (the world as it is) and the phenomenal world (the world as it appears to us). Hick argued that religion is a phenomenal attempt to understand the nature of God, which belongs to the noumenal world. For this reason, all religions fall short of the truth – including Christianity. As a solution,

Hick proposed that doctrines representing Christian 'truth claims' such as the Virgin Birth, should be understood as myths expressing human relationship with the noumenal. From this, Hick argued that a benevolent God would extend His salvation to every good person – not just those who have accepted Christ.

Good technical vocabulary and good to bring in scholarly views. A more direct link to this laying foundations for a pluralist attitude and the extent to which the 'demythologisation' challenges the doctrines would be useful here, to keep the answer on track.

Biblical support for this position comes from James – "you see that a person is considered righteous by what they do and not by faith alone". This is further supported by the focus on good deeds as the path to salvation expressed in the Parable of the Sheep and the Goats in Matthew. Furthermore, in Micah, it is said that the Lord requires us to "act justly and to love mercy and to walk humbly with your God." The ideas that faith is incomplete without moral action and that deeds, not faith alone, are needed for salvation supports the pluralist belief that salvation can be extended to those outside of the Church. The Christian doctrines of God as love, and a time of final judgement can still be upheld by these pluralist beliefs as the focus is on judgement according to action, not faith.

Good linking back to the question, putting the previous paragraph into context and offering Biblical support for this. This shows appropriate selection and use of sources of wisdom and authority, appropriately used to sustain an argument.

However, this position significantly undermines the doctrine of Jesus' death and resurrection which is believed to be of cosmic significance – a fulfilment of God's plan. *Here, the candidate evaluates their own previous argument, showing evidence of a balanced response.* One might also say that this doctrine is more central to Christianity than that of judgement or God's love as Jesus' sacrifice is something that separates Christianity from other Abrahamic religions. *Here, the candidate is showing comprehensive understanding of the demands of the question as they are considering which doctrines are central to Christianity, and not accepting them all at face value.* Jesus taught that he was "the way, the truth and the life" and that "no one gets to the father except through him". The uniqueness of Christ's sacrifice seems to be severely undermined by a pluralist approach that says anyone could potentially be saved. Karl Barth supported this with his 'theology of the Word' – that Christ is the fully unique way God has chosen to reveal himself and so is the only reliable way of gaining knowledge of God. If salvation is extended to anyone, then the Christian doctrines of Jesus as God incarnate (John 1:1) and as a sacrifice for our sins which we are tainted with from the Fall, are severely undermined.

The essay is taking a balanced approach showing strong evaluation and support of the different arguments. The candidate is also being selective about which doctrines are being undermined, showing good knowledge and understanding.

It could be that a broad exclusivist approach could overcome the problems Hick identified of a benevolent God needing to save all. The broad exclusivist approach asserted by D'Costa promotes universal-access exclusivism – that salvation is possible even after death. Although the acceptance of Christ is an integral part of this, this acceptance can happen in the afterlife. 1 Timothy can support such a position – "this is good and pleased God our Saviour, who wants all people to be saved and to come to a knowledge of the truth." If this is what God wants, then it makes sense for it to be possible, since an omniscient and omnibenevolent God could not want for something that could not reasonably be achieved. From this, we might say that theological pluralism undermines Christian doctrines and is also unnecessary as God's love gives non-Christians a chance to turn to Christ in death.

An interesting attempt to critique the basis for pluralism by saying exclusivism can still allow for all to be saved. However, the attempt to link this to the undermining of doctrine is lost.

Theological pluralism also undermines Christian doctrine of 'extra ecclesia nulla salus' – that outside of the Church, there is no salvation. Raimon Panikkar taught life as a 'searching pilgrimage' and a need to be open about the truth rather than making claims about it. He described religious pluralism as a spiritual position, rather than an intellectual one. He argued that God makes himself known to people through Christ – Christophany. This would make Christ 'a way' and not 'the way' to salvation and this should be acceptable because all revelation need interpretation – including the narrative of Jesus' life. Hick would say God can freely make Himself known however He chooses and so salvation can fairly be extended to anyone. If pluralism is a spiritual position, then it could be argued that Christian doctrines are only undermined on an intellectual level and that these doctrines are not as central to Christianity as the spiritual importance of love and righteousness that can be seen in a person's moral life, as opposed to beliefs stated in Creed.

Range of scholars is continued and a good linking of spiritual and intellectual issues with doctrines.

In conclusion, Hick's proposal of demythologisation of the Virgin Birth, creation ex nihilo and the bodily resurrection of Christ and the threat this poses to Christian doctrine begs the question as to which doctrines are central to Christianity. If these doctrines are not taken literally, then it seems that there is little of Christianity left. It seems that theological pluralism not only undermines Christian doctrine but also the work of missionaries and martyrs though the ages. Despite this, the Catholic doctrine of extra ecclesia nulla salus seems to contradict the doctrines of God's omnibenevolence and ability to judge fairly. A 'middle ground' inclusivist approach seems to allow for Christ to remain significant and for the good to be saved. 'Anonymous Christians' who have been unable to freely accept Christ but nevertheless unknowingly follow his example, can be saved (Rahner). Romans seems to support this innate sense for Christ – "they show that the requirements of the law are written on their hearts." The Sheep and the Goats parable also implies that anyone acting out of altruistic love is working for Christ – whether they realise this or not. Therefore, while pluralism poses and intellectual threat to these doctrines, the spiritual threat is not so strong.

Overall: 32/40 80% Grade A

AO1: Level 5 [12]

A very good selection of material. Accurate and appropriate use of a range of technical terms and scholars. The score is 12 rather than 13 as at times, the focus on the precise question is lost a little in the candidates focus on showing knowledge of the scholars.

AO2: Level 5 [20]

Again, good range of scholars and Biblical support and a clear argument which is 'mostly' successful. This does not reach level six because at times, the focus on specific challenge to doctrines is lost. Also, the conclusion seems to mix inclusivism as an ideal, with discussing the threat of pluralism to doctrines. Arts of the conclusion could have appeared earlier on in the argument.

"Christianity follows where culture leads."
Discuss (28/40 Grade B)

Note: this is a question on Secularism (specification area 5)

To say that 'Christianity follows where culture leads' implies that Christian attitudes towards society develop with the changing culture. We might see this today with changing Church rulings on matters of homosexual marriage and the rights of women to become Priests. With a focus on gender, we can see some changes with cultural shift, but to say 'Christianity follows where culture leads' would be an over-generalisation. We might say Christianity continues to engage with changing cultural norms, but this does not mean it changes its doctrines. Indeed, some Christian teachings resist secular views on gender.

A good introduction addressing he implications of the question and signposting the candidate's own ideas without giving too much away. The candidate also draws lines for the scope of the question in this essay with a focus on gender.

Richard Niebuhr, in 'Christ and Culture', provided a study of the extent to which the Church stands inside culture, outside of it, ignores it, stands isolated from it, or transforms it. Niebuhr proposed five views and most of these arguably provide a good framework for addressing the question of the extent to which Christianity follows where culture leads.

A brief paragraph but useful to introduce their choice of bringing in Niebuhr – a promising sign of reading around the specification.

The first of Niebuhr's points, 'Christ against culture', proposes that the Church remains opposed towards culture – a view held by Tertullian. *Could build confidence here by expounding Tertullian so it feels less like a name-drop.* This implies that rather than following the lead of culture, Christianity resists culture's secular values. *Good link back to the question.* For example, Roman Catholics and conservative evangelical Christians are united in believing women's ordination to priests or bishops is wrong. They argue that Christ chose his apostles only from among men; the tradition of the Church in imitating Christ has chosen only men as its leaders; and the living teaching authority (magisterium) has consistently held the exclusion of women from the priesthood as in accordance with God's plan for His Church in first building it on the rock – 'petros' – of St Peter. Pope Francis has recently declared that Pope John Paul II had the final say on women Priests and speaking infallibly, Pope John Paul's words must be binding. He wrote, in 1994 – "the Church has no authority whatsoever to confer priestly ordination on women." This suggests that far from 'following where culture leads', Christianity holds steadfast in its traditions and magisterial reason.

This paragraph shows extensive knowledge of scholars, and makes use of sources of wisdom and authority to develop the line of argument that the Christianity 'resists' rather than 'follows' the lead of culture. Technically strong with appropriate use of specialist vocabulary.

However, it would be an unfair generalisation to apply this Catholic stance to the whole of Christianity. For example, Niebuhr's 'Christ of culture' view attempts to bring culture and Christianity together, despite their differences. *Showing comprehensive knowledge of Niebuhr's work mentioned earlier on. A nuanced approach using this text to framework the essay.* Current examples of this are liberation theology and some feminist theologies. Liberation theology's focus on orthopraxy before orthodoxy makes it a 'theology of action' whereby the kingdom of God is not a place reached upon death; but rather, is something to work for in this life - "[t]he growth of the Kingdom is a process which occurs historically in liberation, insofar as liberation means a greater fulfilment of man" (Gutiérrez). *Excellent use of technical vocabulary and scholars.* Rather than Christianity 'following culture's lead', it seems that Christianity works with

216

culture, in parallel. We can see this in the Church of Scotland allowing same-sex marriage in 2017 and although the Catholic and Anglican Churches still do not allow marriage of same-sex couples, the Anglican Church agreed to debate the issue of blessing civilly partnered homosexual couples in 2017. While slow to progress, it is progress with a cultural lead nevertheless.

Candidate uses examples to develop their use of Niebuhr. The argument has shifted form Christianity resisting culture to Christianity working with cultural change. The candidate remains reluctant to say Christianity 'follows' culture though and so their line of argument continues to develop in a sustained way.

However, it is difficult to see this parallelism in practice. Some argue that Christianity perpetuates injustice by its failure to engage with culture's lead in challenging traditional gender roles. Christianity seems to enforce the subservience of women to men *give examples* and some would say that the principle of agape should instead be used to encourage Christianity to transform with culture to move toward the most loving act – challenging patriarchy and making society fairer. Traditionally, British culture and Church teachings seem to have been aligned in favouring the woman for domestic and maternal roles, and the man for the physical and authoritative roles. Genesis 2 has been highly influential – e.g. "I will make him a helper suitable for him." Woman, supposedly made out of man's rib, will forever be indebted to man in a life of service. The failure of the Catholic Church to ordain women seems to support the resistance of Christianity to cultural leads.

Some insightful comments but not substantiated with scholars and examples. Also, the final comment linking back to the question builds an argument using only Catholicism and not Christianity as a whole. Candidate needs to show that they are not generalising.

However, the 20th century has seen a radical shift in cultural attitudes towards gender. It saw the rights of women to vote in 1928, the Equal Pay Act of 1963 –

giving women the right to be paid the same for doing the same job as men; and the sex discrimination act of 1975 – making it unlawful for men or women to be discriminated against on the grounds of their sex or marital status. Furthermore, there has been a 25% increase of women working since 1950; and single parent families now constitute 25% of the total. These equality laws and the apparent increase in men and women disregarding gender stereotypes, represent a cultural lead in gender and sex equality that Christianity has failed to follow – at least, if we only look at the Catholic and Orthodox churches.

Much better use of knowledge to build an argument here. Statistics given to demonstrate the cultural lead. The comments show the candidate is arguing about a specific group within Christianity and [s]he is aware of this. It would be good to see some contrasting points of Christian groups that appear to have followed this lead however.

The 'Christ and culture in paradox' view is a dualistic view proposing that Christianity belongs to both the spiritual and the temporal realm and must exist in the tension of fulfilling responsibilities to both realms. Furthermore, the 'Christ the transformer of culture' view attempts to convert the principles and goals of secular culture into the service of God's Kingdom. John Wesley and Jonathan Edwards held this view. These last two views seem most aligned with scripture as Christ himself was involved in the transforming of culture without giving prominence to culture. However, a discerning eye is needed. Matthew 16:3 sees Jesus exasperated at the Pharisees – "do you know how to discern the appearance of the sky but cannot discern the signs of the times?" It seems that for Christianity to be building God's Kingdom, it needs, too, to 'discern the times' and this might mean a recognition of what needs transformation and what does not. This is not, then, simply a 'following of culture's lead' since this discernment should not happen without the Logos and Sophia of God.

One example of Christianity following this lead is the decision of the new

Anglican Prayer Book of 1980 to remove the word 'submit' from the marriage vow. The influence of Ephesians 5 on the call to 'submit' in marriage is strong; but the new vow to 'love and cherish' still arguably respects the message in Ephesians 5 to love and respect each other – as in the relationship between Christ and his Church – "for we are members of his body." This part of Ephesians promotes the equality of sexes that we see in the cultural shifts outlined above. Christianity might discern the cultural lead and use its 'sophia' to decide on action.

The above two paragraphs use scripture and a rage of specialist vocabulary to develop the nuanced approach to the question – that Christianity engages with the lead of culture but does not simply 'follow' this lead. Rather, it has to engage with wisdom and the example of Christ to decide on the course of action. Example are used to support this.

In conclusion, Christianity does not 'follow where culture leads'. Rather, it 'transforms from within'. If it merely 'followed' and 'sat comfortably' with secular culture, then it would offer nothing distinctive and would arguably not be worth following. The meaning of the Word of God 'in practice' leads to disagreements, but Christianity arguably sets high standards of moral behaviour that will not be undermined by a pressure to follow the lead of culture.

Overall – 28/40 70% B

AO1: L5 [12]

Very good demonstration of knowledge and understanding. An effective use of Niebuhr to framework the discussion and some use of statistics and sources of wisdom and authority to develop the argument.

AO2: L4 [16]

A nuanced approach suggesting that Christianity works with culture but does not simply 'follow its lead'. In places, the argument was stronger whereas in other places, the candidate focuses on particular groups within Christianity. The 'high standards of moral behaviour' set by Christianity referenced in the conclusion could be brought in earlier.

To what extent do religious experiences provide a basis for belief in God or a higher power? (34/40 Grade A)

Religious experiences can be understood as individual – mystical and conversion; or corporate. The nature of religious experiences has been used as a basis for belief in God. However, religious experiences can also be understood as psychological and physiological phenomena and as such, can be seen to fall short of evidence for the existence of God. While scholars such as Freud and Marx focus on the harmful, illusory nature of religious experiences; others such as William James and Richard Swinburne focus on the authority of the religious experience for the individual. It seems that religious experiences can only ever provide a genuine basis for belief for the experient and cannot provide a basis for belief in the same sense that arguments based on observation (teleological and cosmological) and reason (ontological) can.

Good introduction. It defines the terms of the question and hints at its implications Relevant scholars are introduced and the line of argument is signposted.

Firstly, there are three main sources of knowledge – reason (logical, analytic, a priori); experience (empirical, synthetic, a posteriori) and revelation (authoritative, noetic, divine). Some would argue that religious experiences rely on their own sense of logic ad that they fall outside of the realms of reason and experience. O'Hear would claim that we cannot perform the same 'checks' on religious experiences as we would on other matters such as a test result. This might lead some to believe that if revelation counts as a source of knowledge, then this can only be for the individual as God has selected the experient and revealed something of Himself to them. However, since religious experiences – an experience that is often ineffable – are often characterised by something disembodied; they cannot be used as the basis for a collective belief in God or higher power, since the subject defies both logic and our senses e.g. Mary's revelation from the Angel Gabriel.

This first point introduces different types of knowledge to make the suggestion that religious experiences use their own type of logic and might therefore only count as a basis for belief for the individual. We would expect the candidate to go on to develop this line of argument.

However, one might argue that religious tradition began with religious experiences and in this way, they provide a real basis for a collective belief in God as they have caused individuals to make changes and develop faith. An example is Moses' voice experience. Moses experiences the disembodied voice of God from a burning bush. This was noetic in that God revealed 'I AM that I AM' was his identity. Lastly, the experience was authoritative in that Moses revealed the command to liberate the Israelites from Egypt. St Paul's conversion experience is another example – he experienced Jesus' disembodied voice through a light; the experience was noetic in that Jesus revealed he was the one being persecuted and lastly, it was authoritative as Paul was ordered to go to Ananias and here, was baptised. These individual 'voice' experiences might provide a real basis for belief in God as they brought about a change in the experient. This is transience – one of the four characteristics of religious experience identified by William James. Furthermore, the basis for belief can be seen to extend to beyond that of the individual experient, since both examples involved leadership of the masses.

Good use of key terms and examples and a link to William James that needs to be developed later. The suggestion is made that the basis for belief goes beyond that of the individual – a contrast to the argument signposted earlier. Why is it that a change in the individual can count as evidence of basis of belief? Is this an assumption? This needs a little more explanation.

However, Karl Marx would say that this extension is the 'opiate of the masses' – a form of social control. Marx postulated that the Church used religion as a form of social control to keep people satisfied with their unhappy lives under the promise that the good will be rewarded and the bad punished (seen in the Parable of the Sheep and the Goats, Matthew). He was convinced that Capitalism maintained class division between the rich and poor and that the Church maintained the status quo by promising a better life after death. This can be seen in the Catholic Church's sacrament of reconciliation and the Nicene Creed – "I believe in one baptism for the forgiveness of sins...resurrection of the dead and life everlasting". If religion is no more than a social construct, then religious experiences are no more than a consequence of that construct. This would imply that that religious experiences offer no real basis for belief in God or higher power, since they arise because of the social construct of religious organisation – even Teresa of Avila said that we ought to test the validity of our experiences by seeing if they fall in line with Church Teaching. In this sense, the basis of religious experience for belief in God seems a flawed one.

However, Marx' challenge of the authority of religious experiences is linked to his distrust of the Church as an institution. One could argue that it is unfair to discredit the experience based on the social construct. William James, for example, concluded that the experience should always supersede and come before the institution. The implication of this is that the experience is the basis of the social construct, rather than as result of it. Furthermore, Marx has ignored that for many, religion was much more than an 'opiate' – it is a living aspect of their lives and can be used for social good. William James' example of Nicky Cruz's conversion from gangster to Christian preacher supports this and shows that the religious experience can have a lasting effect on someone's life – transience and in this way, does offer a basis for belief in God or a higher being.

The candidate responds to Marx's criticism effectively and maintains their argument that religious experiences can be a basis for belief in God. Reference to Cruz and scholars makes the argument well-grounded and there are appropriate links made to Church teaching.

Richard Swinburne would identify such individual conversion experiences as private, but describable in ordinary language. The experience would count as authoritative for the individual and point them towards God and a change in life. Furthermore, Richard Swinburne would add credibility to the experience as it would be contradictory to demand empirical evidence for belief and then dismiss it when provided. The only reason we should doubt an account is if we had good reason to doubt the testifier. Since Moses, Paul and Cruz seemed to go on to influence their followers because of their experience, we might count their religious experiences as a genuine testament to God and a firm basis for belief.

Good to see more scholars but the candidate could expand on how influencing others adds to the argument that the experience is a basis for belief. This paragraph seems to be more 'assertion' than grounded reason.

However, O'Hear would argue that we need to perform 'checks' on our experiences as part of our learning. If our experiences cannot be 'checked', then they can be regarded merely as opinion or unscientific. These 'checks' include checks against our other senses, checks across time and checks with 'other checkers' – i.e. can other people validate the experience? The difficulty with religious experiences *Evaluative language, building on implications of the scholar used* is that they cannot be checked in the same way and so cannot be relied upon as evidence for the existence of God. However, one could suggest that the main implication of O'Hear is that religious experiences cannot be used as objective proof for the existence of God. This does not, however, exclude the reality of the authority of the experience for the individual and in this sense, it does offer a basis for belief for the experient.

Links back to the question clearly, building a sustained line of reasoning.

Moreover, William James used mass testimonies as evidence as part of his objective study. James identified four characteristics of religious experience – passivity, ineffability, noeticism and transience and concluded that these experiences superseded any other religious authority such as the church institutions – dogmas, doctrines etc. Some might argue that the validity of religious experiences recorded in the Bible is limited due to their archaism. O'Hear would also say they cannot be 'checked'. *Nice to see James and O'Hear used comparatively.* However, James studied a variety of experiences. Nicky Cruz's experience was passive in that the priest revealed God's love to Nicky; it was ineffable in that Cruz could not understand the affection of the Priest; it was noetic in Cruz's realisation that God loved him and finally, it was transient as Cruz converted from gangster to Christian preacher. *Case study builds strength in knowledge and is used effectively as part of the candidate's approach to the question* James' conclusions can be supported by Friedrich Schleiermacher who said we need faith beyond obedience. Similar to James' conclusion that religious experiences are 'psychological phenomena', Schleiermacher taught that we all have a consciousness for the divine but that we block it off. This could suggest that an individual who has a religious experience should take this seriously and as valid as any other experience. In this sense, the basis for belief in God or a higher power remains.

Range of scholars used critically to build response to the question. Candidate retains strong and precise focus on their understanding of the question. Note the use of linkage words like 'moreover' and 'however' throughout the essay,

However, James' conclusion might still limit the validity of the experience pointing objectively towards a God. James allowed that a person could make themselves more open to religious experiences e.g. through alcohol and drugs as these could bring about a state of relaxed openness such as that achieved by Indian Yoga through mental training. Mackie would say that if religious experiences are psychological, influenced or formulated in the psyche, then they are not divine – they are psychological. In contradiction to James, Mackie argues that if the influence for the experience is the psyche, then they should have no special authority for us. Support for this comes from cases like the Yorkshire Ripper where he claimed a voice from God told him to kill the women. This suggests that some 'religious experiences' might not be a basis for belief at all; but rather, a basis for action and illusion.

Insightful evaluation offering alternative perspective forming part of a balanced approach.

However, Teresa Avilla would say that to know if the experience comes from God, the experience must leave the person with a good disposition and fall in line with Church teaching. Therefore, she would say the Yorkshire Ripper's experience was not religious and so neither should it be used as a basis for belief. However, Mackie's argument that the experience should not have authority for the individual if it is from the psyche seems convincing and supports the argument that the experience might be a basis for belief but this should not extend beyond the individual and should not have authority-especially if its transience effect is going to be negative.

A more nuanced argument building – that the basis for belief may stand for the individual but not beyond.

Lastly, recipients' experiences can be compared to drug induced highs (e.g. Bruce Parry's Iboga root) or to physiological disorders eg. St Paul could have had epilepsy. *Good use of examples and some outside of specification.* This lack of authority for the individual is further supported by Freud's psychological challenge. He said that religious experiences are nothing more than an illusion created by our psyche to satisfy our needs. An example of this is Teresa of

Avila's 'ecstasy' – 'this I thought that he thrust several times into my heart, and that it penetrated to my entrails.' Being a nun, Teresa would have been celibate and so Freud would suggest that this could be her psyche imagining a sexual encounter with a divine object of her devotions. Good engagement of Freud and James with Teresa's experience used as a case example. Rather than being a religious experience providing convincing grounds for belief in God, this experience represents a desire for sexual gratification. Additionally, James believed the experience was the source for the religious traditions; whereas people like Teresa were already a part of a religious tradition. This suggests that the experience is sought after by the experient as opposed to being passive and therefore, it is difficult to claim that the experience is wholly 'passive'. It is difficult to separate the experience from belief or surrounding social influence but it would seem fair to say that for the individual, their experience of the Divine is authoritative and is either a foundation for belief, or strengthens a pre-existing foundation.

In conclusion, it seems that while for the individual, the experience might provide a basis for belief in God and may act as an authority influencing their lives; this foundation should not extend beyond the experient and cannot be tested in the same way as synthetic and analytic knowledge can be. We should not dismiss religious experiences as merely a 'product of the mind' since even if the experience arises from the psyche, it can still bring the experience closer to the Divine 'other' and in this way, remains a basis for belief.

Overall: 34/ 40 85% Grade A

AO1: L6 [14] Focus on the question throughout, accurate use of technical terms and extensive range of scholarly views, accurate and detailed knowledge.

AO2: L5 [20] Clear argument, mostly successful. Successful and clear analysis and evaluation, answers question set. This would be improved by slightly less breadth of material as this can cloud the candidate's own insight and analysis with a focus on the question. Less breadth would allow for a clearer sustained argument – there seems to be some to-ing and fro-ing.

To what extent is Christianity better than Marxism at tackling social issues? (35/40 Grade A)

Social issues include poverty, low literacy and substance abuse. Collectively, social issues seem to stem from a divide in society and an unfair distribution of wealth and power. Christianity can sometimes understand these issues as symptomatic of a world corrupted by human sin and the Fall; while Marxism might understand these issues as symptomatic of alienation due to private ownership of the means of production. The 'best' approach to tackling these social issues will offer practical help for the social issues.

Introduction contextualises the question and shows confident understanding of some Christian and Marxist attitudes. Argument is signposted.

Liberation theology is one Christian attempt to address social issues. It began as an intellectual and practical movement among those working with the poor. Paulo Freire taught 'conscientisation' as the process by which someone becomes aware of the power structures in society and he said that education should teach people to read these structures. Education, for Freire, was not about transmitting information, it should transform society as well. Furthermore, liberation theology advocated orthopraxy (right practice) before orthodoxy (right belief). As a theology of action, liberation theology taught that the Kingdom of God is not a place we reach in death; but something we work for in this life. This could be supported by the Parable of the Sheep and the Goats that focussed on right action – in our treatment of humans, we also respond to God with altruistic love. *Excellent to see liberation theology used here – good links with scholars and technical accuracy regarding orthodoxy and praxis.* James also supports this - "you see that a person is considered righteous by what they do and not by faith alone". Jesus also taught that "whatever you do to the least of these (referring to outcasts), you do to me also". *Links made to sources of wisdom and authority.* These teachings suggest that Christianity is of practical help when dealing with social issues, with charitable acts being a manifestation of the Kingdom of God. By this means, education should be available to all regardless of wealth and gender and those suffering from drug or sexual abuse should be reached out to with love. Such help is seen in Christian charity work such as the work of the Salvation Army in offering specialist detox centres and rehabilitation support programmes working towards social integration. This shows that Christianity can be of practical help in tackling social issues.

It is pleasing to see not only good understanding of some liberation theology but also a link to practical use as seen in the Salvation Army. This shows that the question of social issues is not just being skirted over. The practicality mentioned in the introduction is being focussed on. A contrast with Marx is now needed.

However, it could be said that such social change would not have come without some significant engagement with Marxist ideologies. Marxism taught that with the revolutionization of technology, we have felt less in control. As we became able to produce surplus to requirements, the power favoured those who had control over production. Marx described how we become part of a supply chain - purchasing commodities and not knowing the people involved. In this way, people become alienated from their work and our happiness at cheap prices, comes at the expense of other people's happiness. Christianity similarly focusses on the well-being of each individual, with the added notion that each individual is in God's likeness. Marx's teaching that exploitation occurs when humans are treated as objects and used as a means to an end has resemblance to Kantian ethics, but also falls in line with Christian teaching that every person matters – "there is neither Jew nor Gentile, neither slave nor free, nor is there male and female, for you are all one in Christ Jesus" (Galatians

3:28). Both Marxism and Christianity seem to offer a practical approach to having a concern for the individual as a means of helping to resolve social problems caused by alienation.

Effective tying together of Marxism and Christian teaching, linked straight in with their practical uses.

The liberation theologian Gutierrez warned against using all of Marxism but said that Christianity could benefit from using Marx's theories of alienation and exploitation. For example, he thought that the people of Latin America wanted to be liberated from capitalism and Gutierrez called for the church to stand with such movements for liberation. *Range of scholarly views.* To not get involved in politics would be the same as helping to keep things the same. From this standpoint, being Christian necessitates being political. He taught – "It is a will to build a socialist society, more just, more free, and human, and not a society of superficial and false reconciliation and equality." It could be seen that while Marxism provides more practical help in terms of accessibility for those without a belief in the Divine; Christianity offers a more universal help, keeping in mind that which lies outside of the individual – God. The communism arising from Marx is also less successful since it failed to respond effectively to poverty in the way various Christian charities such as CAFOD and Christian Aid have. For example, communism could not hold back globalisation – seen in China and Cuba opening up to capitalism.

The candidate is developing a stronger line of argument, while continuing to effectively compare and contrast the Christian and Marxist approaches. The CAFOD or Christian Aid point could be developed rather than asserted.

Christianity also tackles social issues better than Marxism since there is a Biblical trend to favour the outcasts and the poor. Jesus teaches – "whatever you did for one of the least of these brothers and sisters of mine, you did for me." This 'preferential option for the poor" shows an authentic Christian response to social issues and puts human dignity central to social work. Allowing social divide to continue is not compatible with the Biblical teachings on peace and justice. However, Segundo differed from Gutierrez by suggesting that liberation from sin should come before social liberation since the latter might not always be possible – even Jesus taught "the poor you will always have with you". While some might argue that Marxism is more successful as Christianity can get lost in orthodoxy before orthopraxy; it could be argued that the Christian offer of salvation, and therefore solace, for the poor – "blessed are the poor in spirit, for their's is the Kingdom of God" - extends real hope for those who suffer. Such solace could not possibly by offered by the secular ideologies of Marxism.

Nice theological link to salvation and how this might offer help beyond just the practical. Good to see even more links with scholars

An interesting Christian perspective comes from Pope Francis who says that we can focus so much on the material world that we end up in a state of spiritual poverty and that this results in a destructive reading of human needs, which in turn results in exploitation of the weak and needy – this is seen in drug and pornography use. *Linked back to social issues.* Cardinal Ratzinger criticised Marxism for being inherently unchristian and denies the 'human person, his liberty, and rights'. Bonaventure criticised liberation theology for focussing too much on structural and not on personal sin. God is the ultimate liberator and liberation theology focusses too much on human action.

This seems like knowledge brought in for the sake of it rather than being used to effectively answer the question/ contribute to argument.

Overall, since inner spiritual change, as well as real action are needed, Christianity can be seen to offer a fuller approach to social issues than Marxism. It would be narrow-minded to suggest that liberation from sin is more important than social liberation; but a concern for the spiritual as well as practical needs of each person is an approach to social issues that Marxism falls short of.

Overall: 35/40 = 88% Grade A

AO1: Level 6 [14]

Excellent range of knowledge and technicality. Candidate effectively compares and contrasts Christian and Marxist thought throughout, rather than dealing with the two ideologies in separate halves. This makes for an effective, sustained and developed argument.

AO2: Level 6 [21]

Views skilfully developed, especially culminating in the concluding comment on the need for spiritual as well as practical help for social issues. More on how Marx could offer practical help for specific social issues (or not) would help to balance out the overall argument and raise the marks.

Critically compare Daly's and Ruether's teaching on God. (29/40 B Grade)

Fundamentally, both Ruether and Daly are trying to promote and subsequently rectify the same issue of gender inequality within Christianity. However, they have rather different perspectives and approaches to the issue as while Ruether focuses on reforming the Church to make it less patriarchal and sexist, Daly holds a more radical and extremist view and is seeking total female dominance. With regard to their teachings on God, it is evident that there are various similarities as they both ultimately disagree with the fact that God is *should be* referenced in male terms, yet on a more specific level they have different goals when it comes to the future of the Church and its teachings on God.

Good introduction but a word like 'extremist' is emotive, not analytical. It is better to refer to the terms post-Christian and radical Christian to refer to the two authors, as Mary Daly argues that a different concept of God is required altogether – hence 'post-Christian', whereas Ruether claims to be able to rediscover an idea of God in Hebrew scriptures (the prophetic tradition eg in Isaiah) which can be salvaged and re-articulated for today.

Firstly, Ruether takes issue with the idea that God is male and believes that this has allowed for the institutionalisation of patriarchy within the Church. According to her, the Church has lost its egalitarian roots as by saying 'God the father' patriarchy is denoted and this seems unjust for women when combined with a view of male headship in the church. Instead, Ruether teaches that we must also address God using some feminine language and she supports this with scripture as often there is the idea of the Goddess as the source of life.

This sentence is muddled because Scripture doesn't refer to God/ess theology at

235

all, this idea comes from pre-Christian religions eg paganism. Note – 'female metaphors for God' is not the same idea as a full-blown God/ess theology, and it is this point which Daphne Hampson makes when she argues that the historical basis of Christianity is 'irreducibly patriarchal 'and cannot be recovered in any other form – Ruether's project is thus fundamentally flawed.

For instance, in Isaiah, God is depicted as a Mother going through childbirth as it says "now I will cry out like a woman in labour". Furthermore, Ruether claims that there is this concept of 'Sophia' in the Holy Spirit as a form of Wisdom, *a reference would be useful here - it is contained in the Wisdom fo Solomon a book of the apocrypha (look up apocrypha)* adding to the need for a female aspect of God. This is somewhat similar to Daly's teaching on God as she believes that a male God has been used to justify the marginalisation and mistreatment of women in the Church and as such this view of God must be changed. *You could make a synoptic link here.* However, Daly takes it one step further in that she believes that God must be castrated and cannot be referred to in either male or female terms, but rather replaced with an authentic human existence. *This authentic existence needs explaining.* She uses terms like "the transvaluation of Christianity" and "female be-ing" to suggest that there is no need for an objective God and in removing him, women will have more power within society. From this, it seems evident that the key difference between these two feminists stems from their diverse attitudes towards men as generally Ruether seeks equality while Daly sees women as the better sex. This is an important criticism of Daly as her teachings on God can be seen to be too exclusive and biased as it promotes lesbian separatism. As a result, one could argue that Ruether's approach is more reasonable as it acknowledges the need for male and female co-operation.

This paragraph is much too long – you need to work on a more sequential and shorter paragraph structure. The transvaluation point needs explanation – the idea is that values of male headship suffuse Scripture and also images of God as Father

Lord and King are all male. The values need to be changed radically and different ones found within Scripture (Ruether) or from outside (Daly) Remember also to keep referring back to the question. To say Ruether's is a more 'reasonable' an approach also needs explaining. Perhaps you could link it to the idea that it is more reasonable to salvage Christianity from the Bible than demolish altogether.

One of Daly's prominent teachings on God is that he forcibly impregnated the Virgin Mary who is "the Total rape" victim. For Daly, this image has legitimised the abuse of women by the Church over the centuries. In addition, she had the view that God had been used to justify the destruction of women's spiritual nature and as such we must break free from this self-imposed cultural imprisonment of religion. Daly puts emphasis on the fact that only women posses the ability to remove these false ideas about God and refers to it as the Apollonian veil which prevents people from accomplishing their creativity and imagination. This is quite dissimilar to Ruether who used argued that theological language referring to God must be based on the apophatic assumption that God is beyond language and therefore gender.

The word 'this' in the previous paragraph (final sentence) is ambiguous. There are a number of ideas and so it's not clear which one 'this' is picking up. Why not make a link to Aquinas theory of natural law - as he argues women are less rational than men and this a divinely designed part of the natural order.

Yet, often theologians tend to use male gendered language to emphasise God's transcendence and female language to emphasise God's immanence. So, while we can use gendered language in analogies and symbols of how humans experience God, Ruether promotes the overall use of more inclusive language. However, it is evident that Ruether did not always stick to this idea as she was more partial to the idea of a Goddess which would compromise the sovereignty of God and reduce the credibility of her teachings. Furthermore, one could argue that she over analyses the situation and perhaps she is making more of an issue than there needs to be.

Another key teaching on God comes from Ruether and addresses the concept of whether or not a male saviour can save women. On the one hand, she argues that with Jesus (the Word of God/Logos) being historically male, women would have to adapt to a male mind set in order to be saved. Similarly, Jesus was promoted as a triumphal king and as a result Churches felt justified in only having male officials who could represent this figure. On the other hand, Ruether believes that salvation was available to women once radical tradition is rediscovered as she suggests that the maleness of Jesus isn't relevant. According to her, we should view Jesus as simply a ruler who sought to restore all human relations, particularly focusing on the marginalised which included women at that time. As a result, it seems clear that Ruether was more interested in how Christianity could be reformed to cater for women. This isn't quite the case for Daly who saw little benefit in reforming the Church as she completely rejects the Catholic Church as fundamentally sexist and patriarchal. This is another key difference between their teachings on God as they have different visions for the future of Christianity.

Daly saw no benefit at all in reforming the church – she agrees with Daphne Hampson that the church is 'irredeemably patriarchal". She calls people to leave the church and describes herself as a 'post-Christian'. The essay needs some critical counterpoints from other authors like Hampson. Good on Ruether. Why not learn a quote from her?

In conclusion, while both feminist theologians are looking to remove the gender inequality within the Church, they have rather different views on how this should be accomplished. They both highlight the idea that in order to gain this social change they need to use extreme measures, however perhaps in Daly's case this has lead to the distortion of her message. Overall, it would seem that Ruether's approach is more equipped to bring about a change in

Christianity regarding equality whereas Daly's approach is somewhat irrational in the way she demonises men, alienating them which ultimately seems counterproductive.

29/40 72% B grade

Interesting essay. I think the lack of a more disciplined paragraph structure upsets the analytical power of the argument and that there are a number of unsubstantiated (inadequately explained) statements/assertions which could do with justifying properly (or eliminating altogether if they don't follow logically). In addition the candidate needs to make more references back to the question. The examiner will also be looking for an additional author to be cited who represents a critical view of both – the obvious one to take is Daphne Hampson. This is clearly an intelligent student who has the potential to gain an A*

AO1 Level 4 (10 marks) A good demonstration of knowledge and understanding. Addresses the question well. Good selection of relevant material, used appropriately on the whole. Mostly accurate knowledge which demonstrates good understanding of the material used, which should have reasonable amounts of depth or breadth. A good range of scholarly views. But the essay needs a counter-argument from, say, Daphne Hampson.

AO2 Level 5 (19 marks) A very good demonstration of analysis and evaluation in response to the question. successful and clear analysis, evaluation and argument. Views very well stated, coherently developed and justified. There is a well–developed and sustained line of reasoning which is coherent, relevant and logically structured.

Appendix 1 The Levels of Assessment

Ao1 – Knowledge And Understanding

An **excellent** attempt to address the question showing understanding and engagement with the material; excellent ability to select and deploy relevant information. Extensive range of scholarly views, academic approaches, and/or sources of wisdom and authority are used to demonstrate knowledge and understanding

Level 5 (11-13 marks)

A **very good** attempt to address the question demonstrating knowledge and understanding. Very good selection of relevant material, technical terms mostly accurate. a very good range of scholarly views, academic approaches, and/or sources of wisdom and authority are used to demonstrate knowledge and understanding

Level 4 (8 -10 marks)

A **good** demonstration of knowledge and understanding. Addresses the question well. Good selection of relevant material, used appropriately on the whole. Mostly accurate knowledge which demonstrates good understanding of the material used, which should have reasonable amounts of depth or breadth. A good range of scholarly views

Level 3 (5 - 7 marks)

A **satisfactory** demonstration of knowledge and understanding with of mostly relevant material. Some accurate knowledge demonstrating understanding through material used but may be lacking in breadth. Sources / academic approaches are used to demonstrate knowledge and understanding with only partial success

Level 2 (3 -4 marks)

A **basic** demonstration of knowledge and understanding in response to the question. Addresses the general topic rather than the question directly. Limited selection of material. Limited use of scholars and key terms.

Level 1 (1 - 2 marks)

A **weak** demonstration of knowledge and understanding in response to the question. Almost completely ignores the question. Very little relevant material or key terminology.

AO2 – Analysis, evaluation and application

Level 6 (21 -24 marks)

An **excellent** demonstration of analysis and evaluation in response to the question. Confident and insightful critical analysis and detailed evaluation of the issue. Views skilfully and clearly stated, coherently developed and justified.

Excellent line of reasoning, well-developed and sustained, which is coherent, relevant and logically structured.

Level 5 (17-20 marks)

A **very good** demonstration of analysis and evaluation in response to the question. successful and clear analysis, evaluation and argument. Views very well stated, coherently developed and justified. There is a well–developed and sustained line of reasoning which is coherent, relevant and logically structured.

Level 4 (13-16 marks)

A **good** demonstration of analysis and evaluation in response to the question. Generally successful analysis, evaluation and argument. Views well stated, with some development and justification. Answers the question set well. There is a well–developed line of reasoning which is clear, relevant and logically structured.

Level 3 (9 -12 marks)

A **satisfactory** demonstration of analysis and/evaluation in response to the question. Some successful argument. Partially successful analysis and evaluation. Views asserted but often not fully justified. Mostly answers the set question. There is a line of reasoning presented which is mostly relevant and which has some structure.

Level 2 (5 - 8 marks)

A **basic** demonstration of analysis and evaluation in response to the question. Only partially answers the question. Some analysis, but not successfully justified. views asserted but with little justification. There is a line of reasoning which has some relevance and which is presented with limited structure.

Level 1 (1 - 4 marks)

A **weak** demonstration of analysis and evaluation in response to the question. Very little argument or justification of viewpoint, little or no successful analysis Communication: often unclear or disorganised.

Checklist for Self-assessment

AO1 Criteria - Knowledge and Understanding

1. Have I used a broad range of scholars (some supporting, some opposing my thesis) relevant to answering this question? Is this range appropriate (meaning not too many nor too few, and the relevant scholars and views?)

2. Have I demonstrated a very clear focus on this question by producing a thesis statement either at the beginning or as a conclusion (or both)?

3. Have I shown understanding by not just asserting, but analysing a viewpoint by using link words like 'because' and 'in order to'?

4. Have I exposed one or two assumptions behind a scholar's or philosopher's view point and made allusion tot eh worldview that governs these assumptions?

5. Have I avoided lists which are simply learned off by heart and then reproduced?

AO2 Criteria - Analysis and Evaluation

1. Have I built upon my knowledge by showing linkages between ideas?

2. Have I used paragraphs of about equal length which move through a structure of thought, one paragraph building on or contrasting with the last one?

3. Have I fully developed my main points by using analytical words or phrases like "moreover" and "furthermore".

4. Have I fully evaluated as I go along (and not just tacked this on as an

afterthought) using such evaluative words and phrases as "however", "this assumes that", "X disagrees that Y (or with Y)...because", "it is arguably invalid to argue".

5. Have I produced a strong conclusion which clearly follows from what goes before? Have I made sure I don't tack extra thoughts on at the end (which I haven't had time to develop)?

6. Have I made synoptic links with other parts of the course where relevant?

7. Have I used my own (or other scholars') examples where appropriate (and tried not to use the textbook ones which almost everyone else will be using)?

8. Could I reproduce the question at the top if I removed the question altogether?

Revision Access Website

Opening March 25th 2018

Our unique guides provide you with a special benefit - your own revision site which is fully integrated with the guides and only available to purchasers.

All our revision materials for Christian Thought, Ethics, and Philosophy of Religion are available to each purchaser of any individual guide. Resources include model essay samples found at the back of each chapter, and also:

- Articles
- Extracts
- Handouts
- Roadmap
- Summary
- Videos
- Whizz Through Powerpoints

Visit: peped.org/revision-access

Printed in Great Britain
by Amazon